SHORT BIKE RIDES
NEW JERSEY

"*Short Bike Rides in New Jersey* is a collection of 30 bike tours, none longer than 25 miles. . . . Mr. Santelli has also provided cultural and sightseeing information. Included are tours of varying difficulty, maps, as well as equipment and safety information."
—*New York Times*

"The tours are divided among five regions, Northern New Jersey, Western New Jersey, Central New Jersey, The Jersey Shore, and Southern New Jersey, and each includes a basic tour description, tips, and maps."
—*Mid-Atlantic Country*

"Santelli's style incorporates straight information about bike routes with anecdotes and other tidbits."
—*Asbury Park Press*

"There are easy to read sketch maps accompanying each suggested route, and comprehensive directions."
—*Pike County* (PA) *Dispatch*

Merry Christmas
1992
Love — Cindy

Other Books by Robert Santelli:

Aquarius Rising: The Rock Festival Years

The Big Beat: Conversations with Rock's Great Drummers, co-authored with Max Weinberg

Sixties Rock: A Listener's Guide

The Jersey Shore: A Travel and Pleasure Guide

SHORT BIKE RIDES IN NEW JERSEY

Second Edition

by Robert Santelli

An East Woods Book

The Globe Pequot Press

Chester, Connecticut

Library of Congress Cataloging-in-Publication Data

Santelli, Robert.
    Short bike rides in New Jersey / by Robert Santelli. — 2nd ed.
        p.   cm.
    "An East Woods book."
    ISBN 0-87106-196-1
    1. Bicycle touring—New Jersey—Guidebooks.   2. New Jersey—Description and travel—1981—Guidebooks.   I. Title.
GV1045.5.N5S26   1992
796.6'4'09749—dc20
                                                91-45083
                                                CIP

Maps by Cindy Kraft

This book is printed on recycled paper.
Manufactured in the United States of America
Second Edition / First Printing

For Jenna

Acknowledgments

This book could not have been written without the generous help and support of William Feldman, Bicycle Advocate, New Jersey Department of Transportation; Eileen Thornton, New Jersey Department of Commerce and Economic Development, Division of Travel and Tourism; the New Jersey Bicycle Council; Steve Oliphant and the Bicycle Touring Club of North Jersey; Sandy Choron; Ann Sorrel; Dorothea Kraft; Sally McMillan, Donna Carey, Kate Siegel Bandos, Kevin Lynch, Bruce Markot, Laura Strom, and Linda Kennedy of The Globe Pequot Press; Kathy Michalove; Hunterdon County Park System; Pro-Tour Cycles of Westfield; and my daughters, Jaron and Jenna, and my son, Jake.

A special thanks is due my wife and partner, Cindy, who spent many hours drawing up the maps to my bike tours when she could have been happily paging through mail-order catalogues. Finally, a warm, extra-special thanks goes to Wayne Hartman, my mentor and close friend. His advice, encouragement, and love mean much to me. His influence can be found on every page of this book.

Contents

Introduction 1
The Basics of Bicycle Touring 5
Ten Touring Tips 9

NORTHERN NEW JERSEY
1. Ringwood Roundabout 11
2. Ringwood Ramble 17
3. Swartzwood Lake Loop 23
4. Delaware Water Gap 29
5. Old Mine Road Run 33
6. Jockey Hollow 39
7. Great Swamp Swing 45

WESTERN NEW JERSEY
8. Tour of Tewksbury 49
9. Round Valley Ramble 55
10. Flemington Flow 59
11. Stockton—Covered Bridge Tour 65
12. Lambertville Loop 71
13. Washington Crossing State Park 77

CENTRAL NEW JERSEY
14. Cheesequake State Park 83
15. Highlands Hilltopper 89
16. Navesink River Ramble 93
17. Holmdel Hustle 97
18. Monmouth Battlefield 103
19. Allaire 109

THE JERSEY SHORE
20. Sandy Hook 115
21. The Barnegat Peninsula 121
22. Island Beach State Park 127
23. Long Beach Island North Loop 133
24. Long Beach Island South Loop 139

SOUTHERN NEW JERSEY
25. The Pine Barrens 143
26. The Lumberton–Vincentown Loop 147
27. The Jersey Devil Run 153
28. Brigantine National Wildlife Refuge 159
29. Victorian Cape May 163
30. Cape May Point Pedal 169

Introduction

Bicycling has been a part of my life for as long as I can remember. As a kid, my ten-speed was always more than a means to get me downtown or to the park. It was my first real symbol of freedom. It allowed me to explore the town I lived in as well as those communities that surrounded it. My bike gave me the chance to be on my own whenever I rode it. It also translated into responsibility, and, in general, growing up.

As a teen, despite getting my driver's license and a car to commute to college, my bicycle remained a main means of transportation and exploration. After college, I toured Europe on a bike I bought in London, and from then on I knew intimately the immense rewards of bicycle touring. I have since bicycled throughout much of the United States, parts of Central America, Iceland, and Canada on my Claud Butler. As a journalist, I have written much about my travels and the art of bicycle touring. Today, it's a rare trip I take that doesn't include my ten-speed.

But when I told my bicycling buddies of my plans to compile a book of bicycle tours in New Jersey, they were surprised. Why, they asked, would I want to write about bicycling in New Jersey when there were so many other places to map and describe in a bicycle tourbook?

My answer to them was twofold. I chose New Jersey because it is my home and because I've cycled in just about every region of it. I told them that writing a book such as *Short Bike Rides in New Jersey* was a way of accumulating all things pleasant that I've seen, felt, and experienced on Jersey roads into one tidy volume. In a way, I saw the book as a payback of sorts for all those memorable miles and the many more, I hope, that are in store for me and my family in the future.

The second part of my answer was less nostalgic and less personal. And it certainly was more surprising to my cycling friends than the first part of the answer. New Jersey, I said, is a fine state to tour and to explore on a bicycle. I meant it. True, it has many cities and many city-like suburbs, few of which lend themselves to bicycle touring. But New Jersey also has the Shore, the mountains, the Pine

Barrens, farmlands, forests, gently rolling hills, lazy country roads, and a state park system ideally suited for cycling. And the best thing about all of these is their accessibility. You don't have to travel that far to get to Cape May, for instance, even if you do live in northern New Jersey or New York.

The main focus of this book is *short* bike rides. There are important reasons why I've not included any tours exceeding twenty-five miles. Other bicyclists have authored books on bicycle touring in New Jersey. But virtually all of these books comprise longer, more extensive tours, aimed primarily at the more qualified cyclist. He is the one who can accomplish fifty or sixty miles in one day and who can keep a steady pace from start to finish.

Short Bike Rides in New Jersey was written with the less zealous, weekend bicycle rider in mind. All of the tours included in *Short Bike Rides* are twenty-five miles long, or shorter. Every ride ends in the spot where it began, even if the ride is not exactly in the form of a loop. Most can be completed in one to two hours. Each ride includes a number of sights to see and things to do along the way. A half or full day's worth of activities and fun can be built around each tour.

Short Bike Rides in New Jersey was also written with the hope of reaching as many touring cyclists as possible in this state and neighboring ones. I tried to keep in mind the needs and expectations of the young cyclist and his older counterpart, the novice as well as the veteran rider.

Few cyclists who are in fair physical shape will find the tours contained in this book too difficult or too demanding to complete. Yet there is just enough challenge built into nearly all of them for you to know at the end of the day that your body got some exercise and stimulation.

Some tours are more strenuous than others. Less confident cyclists might wish to select those tours for which the terrain is labeled "flat" and the total mileage is less than ten. Those cyclists looking for more variety in terrain might prefer the tours that include hills.

If there is a theme to *Short Bike Rides in New Jersey*, it is for the reader/cyclist to see the state and as many natural, man-made, and historical treasures as possible. I am convinced that the best way to experience any area is on bicycle. The thousands of miles I've logged in over ten years of touring has taught me the value of pedaling to a destination instead of driving to it. If you complete every tour in this book, you will have seen much of what is special about New Jersey. You will also become an experienced bicycle tourist, to boot.

I tried to include tours from all parts of the state in *Short Bike Rides*. However, there are certain urban counties such as Hudson, Union, and Essex that are so densely populated and the roads so heavy with traffic that such a goal was impossible to achieve. Be forewarned, however. Not every tour in *Short Bike Rides* consists of traffic-free roads. That, too, was an impossible goal to accomplish. New Jersey is a small state; it ranks near the bottom in total square miles. And even though 40 percent of New Jersey is forest land, it still is the most densely populated state in the union.

Thus, one should obey all traffic laws when cycling, should adhere to the safety guidelines presented in the "Basic Bicycle Safety" section, which follows this Introduction, and should always ride with caution.

There are few tours for Southwestern New Jersey. Although the area has many good cycling roads, is sparsely populated, and undoubtedly possesses its share of natural beauty, there were few good routes around which to design short bike tours if I remained true to my original intentions; create tours that have a number of things to do and see along the way.

I also tried to devise unique tours to already-discovered New Jersey bicycling areas. I strove to find new roads around familiar attractions. I believe I often succeeded. Where I did not, I used parts of existing tours that were available to me and that met the general guidelines of this book. Where entire tours were used, credit has been given to the appropriate bicycle club or government agency.

Every effort has been made to ensure accuracy of both the directions and the maps of each tour. I rode every tour in the book twice: once on my bicycle and once in a car. Cindy Kraft, my illustrator (also my wife), participated the second time around. We tried to make the maps and the words that embellish them as simple and

3

as straightforward as possible. Only you, the touring cyclist, will know if we did a good job.

Bicycle touring can be enjoyed almost any time of the year in New Jersey. Spring, summer, and fall are certainly better than winter for obvious reasons. The best time to complete the bike tours near or at the Shore would be, of course, summer. But don't discount fall, especially September, since there is much less traffic on Shore roads then, and you still have air and water temperatures warm enough for a dip in the ocean.

Spring and fall are fine seasons to complete the other tours, although Jersey springs are apt to be wet. Fall is a wonderful season for cycling in New Jersey. By all means, experience the tours in north, northwest, and western New Jersey in late September, October, or early November. It is then that the trees are awash in color. Such a spectacle will make your ride that much more rewarding and memorable.

A few words about how to use this book: Read through the directions to each tour and become familiar with the maps before you begin. You will save a lot of "stop and go" time. Then, out on the road, refer to the simplified set of directions included with each tour.

I also recommend that you have a quality handlebar pannier, preferably with a see-through plastic shield under which maps and books like this one may be kept. A simple glance at the map and directions will be all you need from time to time if you follow my advice and become familiar with your chosen tour prior to setting out. And whenever the directions and map are more comprehensive and dictate a more careful, detailed look, having the book close at hand is more convenient than searching through a stuffed backpack or rear pannier.

Enough said. Now it's time to tour. Select one tour that tickles your fancy and be off. Have as much fun completing the tours in this book as I did researching, riding, and ultimately writing about them.

Happy cycling.

The Basics of Bicycle Touring

Bicycle touring requires more than a bike and scenic roads. You need to do some advanced planning. You need the right kinds of equipment and clothing to make your tour, no matter what the distance or difficultly, a pleasant one. By reading through this book and selecting a tour, you've already begun the preparation stage.

Carefully read through the tour you choose at least twice. Take into account the mileage, the region of New Jersey it passes through, the terrain, and the attractions along the way. Be certain it is a tour you will be able to complete—and enjoy.

The second part of the preparation stage is making sure your bike is road-ready. The easiest way to spoil a day on the road, aside from bad weather or excess traffic, is a mechanical breakdown. Eliminate the potential for broken spokes, malfunctioning brakes and derailleurs, and flat tires by having a reputable bicycle mechanic check over your bike before you depart. No one, of course, can guarantee every tour to be hassle-free, but a thorough tune-up will at least minimize bicycle breakdowns.

Most bicycle tourists who never venture off the road need only a standard ten-speed bike to complete the tours in this book. Although mountain or all-terrain bikes are popular, they are unnecessary for the kind of touring outlined in *Short Bike Rides*. Mountain bikes are rugged machines, specifically suited for terrains other than smooth road surfaces.

(*Note:* There is one tour in which a mountain bike is preferred over a traditional ten-speed. That tour is the Brigantine National Wildlife Refuge Loop. It has a rough, gravel surface, perhaps a problem for ten-speeds and their skinny tires, but a cinch for mountain bikes and their fat, knobbed tires. Other tours have some stretches where the cyclist must proceed with caution due to a rough road surface.)

Most experienced cyclists know that toe clips (or toe straps), those funny-looking foot cages attached to the pedals, make the pedaling process more efficient. The energy spent getting from one point to another on a bicycle taxes your leg muscles. It makes sense, then, to spread the pedaling task over as many leg muscles as possible. Riding with toe clips will help you become a better bicycle rider and cut down on leg fatigue when touring.

Fenders are also a good idea. You'll most appreciate them when the roads are wet. Fenders will keep you drier and cleaner. If you don't pretend to be a bike racer when touring, the extra weight of a front and rear fender is so small that it will not trouble you.

Water bottles are a must for obvious reasons. Two are better than one, especially during warm weather. Keep one bottle in the water bottle bracket attached to your bike frame. Keep the other in your saddlebag or pannier.

You will need something to carry a camera, some snacks, sunglasses, and other personal items. A front handlebar pannier should suffice. You can store maps and this book in a waterproof pannier and a see-through plastic shield. There are many panniers and packs on the market. Be choosey.

So much for tour planning and bicycle preparation. What about equipment to bring with you on the road? You certainly don't want a bike loaded down with unnecessary gear. Travel light. However, there are a few essentials that you will be glad you brought along should something go wrong.

Like tools. A toolbag and some basic tools are a must. Bring what you think you might need. Certainly an adjustable crescent wrench (4-inch or 6-inch), a small pliers, an Allen wrench set, a screwdriver, and at least two tire irons are mandatory. So is a tire patch kit. And don't forget a pocket knife and a compact, easy-to-use bicycle repair book. A spoke wrench, a freewheel tool, and a chain tool are wise to bring if you know how to use them. Also in the toolbag might be an extra brake cable (rear), six extra spokes, an extra brake pad, and a spare tire tube.

If you get a flat, you'll be glad you brought along an air pump that works. If you misjudge dusk and darkness, a small portable light will come in handy. A lock and cable are a necessity if you plan to leave your bike for any period of time. A safety flag enables cars to see you and adjust their speed and road position.

Fashion has become a big part of the bicycle clothing industry lately. Bicyclists want to look good on the road. There is nothing wrong with that; however, there is something wrong when fashion becomes the only point of comparison when selecting a riding outfit. A bicycle tourist can accomplish any tour in this book wearing a pair of jeans or shorts, a pair of sneakers, a shirt, and, depending on the weather, a jacket or sweatshirt. But if you plan to take bicycle touring seriously and hope to ride fairly often, it is smart to invest in a few garments that will surely make your ride more comfortable.

A good pair of cycling shorts, for instance, is a wise investment. Select a pair with a chamois-lined crotch to absorb sweat. Also, make certain the shorts are long enough to prevent chafing on your inner thighs. Cotton, wool, or polypropylene are better than nylon or polyester shorts.

Another good investment is a pair of cycling shoes. If you only stick to the type of tours in this book, you will not be doing much extensive, long-distance riding. Select a shoe that is lightweight and comfortable, yet thick-soled. You'll be making stops along the way to visit museums and other attractions, so stay away from cleated shoes. They are almost impossible to walk in comfortably. You want versatility in your cycling shoes—you will need to walk as well as ride in them.

Bold, bright-colored cycling shirts are very popular—and a good idea. A driver is more apt to spot you on the road if you wear bright clothing while touring. These shirts, though, are usually expensive. Cyclists not ready to shell out sixty dollars or so might look for a simple, yet colorful, cotton shirt. A long-sleeved shirt is a good idea for early morning rides. Thin layers of clothing are always better than bulk, they keep you warmer and may be removed individually if necessary.

A lightweight, easy-to-stuff windbreaker, preferably one made of Gore-Tex, is another sound investment. There are many cheap windbreakers on the market—you get what you pay for. Don't skimp here. A quality Gore-Tex windbreaker is waterproof, yet it allows air to circulate so you don't become soaked with perspiration. You can use such a windbreaker not only for cycling but for other outdoor activities too. The only drawback to a Gore-Tex windbreaker: the price. A good one may cost a hundred dollars.

Forget about those cute cycling caps bicycle racers wear. Do yourself a favor and opt for a helmet. Buy the best one you can afford. Your helmet could save your life. Find out how well the helmet you select will protect your head in a serious spill. Ask questions about its design and get answers before you reach for your wallet.

It pays to do a bit of research on what constitutes a quality helmet. Once again, there are lots of helmets on the market. Check the consumer section of the bicycling periodicals found at your local newsstand for the latest information on the newest helmets and helmet design.

Gloves with padded leather palms will help prevent your hands from hurting on longer tours. Holding onto the handlebar can get tedious and tiresome. Make sure the finger openings on the gloves you buy are not so tight that they hinder blood circulation. Cycling gloves should fit snugly.

Try to avoid riding in the rain. It's dangerous and not very rewarding. But if you do get caught in a downpour, you'll be glad you brought along a rain cape or poncho. A good alternative to a cape or poncho is your Gore-Tex windbreaker. It won't cover you like a cape, but at least the upper part of your body will stay dry while you search for shelter.

Ten Touring Tips

If you bought this book, you undoubtedly know how to ride a bicycle. But pedaling to the store or to the railroad station is a bit different than completing a twenty-five-mile tour of a section of New Jersey's countryside.

Here are ten touring tips to keep in mind when you ride. They will help you grow from a novice bicycle tourist into an experienced one:

1. If you ride a bike on New Jersey roads, you must obey traffic laws. *Stop* at stop signs and red traffic signals. Take a defensive position when passing through "yield" intersections, amber traffic signals, and high traffic areas. Ride with traffic, never against it.

2. When riding in residential areas or towns, beware of pedestrians, car doors suddenly opening, and cars pulling out of driveways. On rural roads, keep a sharp eye out for dogs.

3. When riding on major thoroughfares, stay inside the shoulder area. If there isn't a designated shoulder, imagine there is one, and ride within its boundaries.

4. Always be on the lookout for rocks, broken pavement, oil slicks, wet leaves, glass, and loose gravel. Hitting any of this debris could cause you to spill or give your bike a flat tire.

5. Pace yourself and don't be afraid to take frequent rests. Bicycle touring is supposed to be fun. If you push yourself too hard, you'll miss the scenery and the serenity that touring offers the cyclist.

6. Don't wait until you're thirsty to drink. Don't wait until you're hungry to snack.

7. Use the gears on your bike efficiently. Low gears are for going up hills; high gears are for coming down. Flat terrain requires a gear in between. According to Bike Centennial, a popular bicycle touring organization, a "brisk, steady cadence of 65–80 pedal revolutions per minute" equals proficient cycling.

8. If you're touring with a companion, practice the cycling technique of drafting, especially in headwinds. Here is how it works: The lead rider cuts wind resistance for the rider(s) behind. The second rider in the draft should stay approximately one to two feet from the lead rider's rear tire. The second rider should also stay a half foot to the right of the lead rider. Communication is important when drafting. The lead rider must relay information to the rider(s) behind him concerning traffic, turns, road debris, and other road hazards.

9. Make sure your brakes are in working order before any ride, but especially rides which contain hills. When braking, apply equal pressure to front and rear brakes.

10. Whenever you leave your bike, even if it's only for a moment, lock it. Don't forget to take your handlebar pannier with you. If you don't, its contents might not be there when you return.

1. Ringwood Roundabout

County: Passaic
Number of Miles: 15.1
Degree of Difficulty: Moderate to difficult
Terrain: Many hills
Surface: Good
Things to See: Ringwood State Park, Skylands Manor, Skylands Botanical Garden, Shepherd Lake, Ringwood Manor and Museum

Some years ago I was assigned by *New Jersey Monthly* magazine to rate and write about the state parks of New Jersey. It was a difficult but rewarding assignment. I had to visit all the state parks and then judge each of them. I took into consideration what they had to offer (activities, museums, special events, etc.) as well as general upkeep and overall beauty.

Of the twenty-five state parks (not including state forests) that I visited and described in the article, I rated Ringwood number one. There have been many improvements made to New Jersey's state park system since that article appeared in 1980. But after returning to many of New Jersey's state parks to put together bike tours for this book, I found Ringwood still rates at the top or at least in the top three. (Other big favorites of mine are Island Beach and Washington Crossing. Both have bicycle tours worth riding. See the Shore and Central Jersey sections of this book.)

This tour is a hilly one, and part of it is on a major thoroughfare. There was no getting around the hills or Greenwood Lake Turnpike (Route 511 North), however. Thus, Ringwood Roundabout might not be a tour for the novice bicycle tourist to try first even though it appears first in this book. Complete some of the easier tours, gain some road experience, and tune up your leg muscles enough so that climbing hills isn't a disagreeable task. Then Ringwood Roundabout can be enjoyed, and its many sites, both natural and historical, can be truly appreciated.

The tour begins in the Ringwood Plaza parking lot. Exit the plaza and make a left onto Skyline Drive. A few hundred yards

How To Get There: Garden State Parkway, Exit 154, to Route 46 West. Route 46 West to Route 23 North. Route 23 North to Route 511 North. Route 511 North to Skyline Drive in Ringwood. Ringwood Plaza, the tour's starting point, is on Skyline Drive.

RINGWOOD ROUNDABOUT: DIRECTIONS AT A GLANCE

1. Left out of Ringwood Plaza and onto Skyline Drive.
2. Right onto Greenwood Lake Turnpike.
3. Right onto Skylands Road.
4. Enter Skylands Manor Section of Ringwood State Park.
5. Right at first intersection in park.
6. Bear right at yield sign.
7. Bear right at fork. Follow signs for Botanical Gardens.
8. After visiting Botanical Gardens head toward Shepherd Lake.
9. Bear right at fork in road.
10. Proceed through two gates.
11. Left at stop sign.
12. Bear right and make left onto Lake Entrance Road.
13. Make left at stop sign onto Route 72 (New York).
14. Right into entrance of Ringwood Manor Section of Ringwood State Park.
15. After visiting Manor House, right back onto Sloatsburg Road (formerly Route 72).
16. Left at stop sign onto Greenwood Lake Turnpike.
17. Left onto Skyline Drive.
18. Right into Ringwood Plaza.

away, you'll come to a stop sign and a dangerous intersection. Go straight after passing the stop sign, but do so with caution. Proceed down Skyline Drive to another stop sign, this one at the Greenwood Lake Turnpike intersection. Make a right and ride north on Greenwood Lake Turnpike. On your left is the Wanaque Reservoir. Stay as far to the right of the road as possible, since the speed limit is fifty miles per hour and there are no shoulders.

About two miles up the road you'll come to the turn-off for Skylands Road. Bear right onto Skylands Road and begin your climb to the south entrance of the Skylands Manor Section of Ringwood State Park.

A mile and a half up on Skylands Road you'll come to a gate that, in the summer, is usually closed. The gate is there to keep out cars, not bicycles, so ride around it. You are now in the Skylands Manor Section of Ringwood.

You'll soon come to an intersection. Make a right and follow a flat, pleasant road with small ponds, fields, and trees on both sides of it. One section of the road is a tree tunnel. The trees are so close to the road and so large that their highest branches extend over it and form a beautiful canopy.

You'll eventually come to a yield sign. Bear right. Next up is a small hill and a fork in the road. Bear right and follow the signs for Skylands Manor Botanical Gardens. Fifty yards or so ahead, pass through another gate. Just beyond the gate bear left. Skylands Manor and the Botanical Gardens, your first stop, are up ahead.

The public is no longer permitted inside Skylands Manor, but an examination of the wonderful architectural detail of this mid-1920s mansion, designed by renowned architect John Russell Pope, is recommended. Skylands Manor is made of gray granite extracted from the nearby Ramapo Mountains. It has forty-five rooms, many of which are being restored. The state has plans to use the manor as a conference center someday.

Across the way is the Manor's Carriage House, now a small visitor's center and headquarters of the Skylands Association, a nonprofit organization that maintains the manor's gardens as well as the Botanical Gardens.

Visitors are permitted to stroll through the Botanical Gardens. Lock up your bike and do just that. Pick up a free map of the gardens at the Visitor's Center and take in the sights and smells of one of Ringwood's most popular attractions. The Botanical Gardens comprise many small gardens. If you're interested in horticulture, you'll want to spend more time here than the average visitor.

After your visit to the Botanical Gardens, proceed further into the park toward Shepherd Lake. Soon you'll come to a fork in the road. Bear right and ride to the stop sign about fifty yards away. Go through the stop sign intersection and through another gate. About a mile down the road (none of the roads have names or markers, by the way), you'll come to yet another gate. Go through the gate and continue to the next stop sign where you'll make a left, then bear right, then make another left onto Lake Entrance Road. All of this happens rather quickly.

Two hundred feet down the road, you'll pass a small tollbooth. Continue down Lake Entrance Road to its end. At the stop sign intersection, you'll make a left and leave the park. You are no longer in New Jersey, either, but New York State. Proceed down the hill on Route 72 and be wary of fast-moving traffic. When you cross the border a few miles down the road and are back in New Jersey, this road becomes Sloatsburg Road. Continue on Sloatsburg Road to the entrance of Ringwood Manor, your next stop.

Make a right back into Ringwood State Park. This section is called Ringwood Manor since it includes the famous Manor House. This National Historic Landmark and former home of such noted families as the Coopers and Hewitts is open to the public. Peter Cooper is best known as a wealthy New York philanthropist and the founder of Cooper Union Institute. Abraham Hewitt was a nine-teenth-century ironmaster who supplied much of the area with iron products. Inside the Manor House are relics from the iron-making days at Ringwood and collections of antiques and period pieces. Visitors can also view a deck gun from "Old Ironsides," America's famous naval vessel.

The Manor House is not, however, open year-round. It opens in the spring and closes the end of October. Plan your trip accordingly.

After your tour of the Manor House and museum is over, proceed back out the entrance/exit of Ringwood Manor. Bear right and continue south on Sloatsburg Road. Approximately four miles later you'll come to a "T" intersection and stop sign. Make a left here onto

Greenwood Lake Turnpike. Follow the Turnpike back to the intersection of Skyline Drive. On your right will be the Wanaque Reservoir. Pass the Skylands Road intersection where you originally turned off to ride into the Skylands Manor Section of Ringwood State Park. Continue on Greenwood Lake Turnpike until Skyline Drive. You'll know you're there when you spot the island at the base of Skyline Drive in the middle of the road and the flagpoles flying the American flag and flag of New Jersey. Make a left onto Skyline Drive and follow it back to Ringwood Plaza where the tour concludes.

Note: This Tour is provided through the courtesy of Steven Oliphant and the Bicycle Touring Club of North Jersey.

2. Ringwood Ramble

County: Passaic
Number of Miles: 20
Degree of Difficulty: Difficult
Terrain: Some hills
Surface: Good
Things to See: Wanaque Reservoir, back roads of Ringwood and New Milford Township, Wanaque Wildlife Management Area

Like the Ringwood Roundabout, this tour also originates out of Ringwood Plaza. Although the tour contains some hills, they are not the reason Ringwood Ramble is judged "difficult". The rating has to do with the roads. Few of them have spacious shoulders where touring cyclists can ride comfortably and without competing for roadspace with cars. Thus, the cyclist must take special caution on those tour roads where the speed limit is above thirty-five miles per hour.

Don't let this discourage you, though. This tour was built around a longer, more comprehensive tour of Ringwood and West Milford's back roads frequently used by the Bicycle Touring Club of North Jersey. Because of the rural nature of this part of Passaic County, almost none of the roads have the kind of wide, well-paved shoulders found in other sections of the state.

To start the tour, exit the Ringwood Plaza parking lot and make a left onto Skyline Drive. A few hundred yards away, you'll come to a stop sign and a dangerous intersection. Go straight after passing the stop sign, but do so with caution. Proceed down Skyline Drive to a second stop sign, this one at the Greenwood Lake Turnpike intersection. Make a left and ride south on Greenwood Lake Turnpike. On your right is the Wanaque Reservoir.

About a mile and a half from the point you turned onto the turnpike is West Brook Road. Make a right on West Brook. This is a snug road, and there are a few tight bends, so ride with caution. The view of the southern section of the Wanaque Reservoir, however, is splendid.

GREENWOOD LAKE TPK.

MARSHALL HILL RD.

Wanaque River

Carpi Lk.

MORSETOWN RD.

Wanaque Reservoir

Kitchell Lake

SKYLINE DR.

START
STOP

GREENWOOD LAKE TPK.

MAGEE RD.

Swamp

STONETOWN RD.

WEST BROOK RD.

Reservoir

N

How To Get There: Garden State Parkway, Exit 154, to Route 46 West. Route 46 West to Route 23 North. Route 23 North to Route 511 North. Route 511 North to Skyline Drive in Ringwood. Ringwood Plaza, the tour's starting point, is on Skyline Drive.

RINGWOOD RAMBLE: DIRECTIONS AT A GLANCE

1. Left out of Ringwood Plaza onto Skyline Drive.
2. Left onto Greenwood Lake Turnpike.
3. Right onto West Brook Road.
4. Bear Right at "island" onto Stonetown Road.
5. Left just beyond Ringwood Boro Fire House onto Magee Road.
6. Right back onto West Brook Road.
7. Right onto Morsetown Road.
8. Right onto Marshall Hill Road, which becomes Greenwood Lake Turnpike.
9. Greenwood Lake Turnpike to Skyline Drive.
10. Left onto Skyline Drive to Ringwood Plaza.

You'll come to an "island" in the middle of West Brook Road about a mile or so later. Bear right. You'll now be on Stonetown Road. Proceed on Stonetown Road until you see the Ringwood Boro Fire House on your left. Just beyond the fire house is Magee Road. Turn left onto Magee Road.

You'll ride over a small bridge and remain on Magee Road until the "T" intersection. Make a right at the "T" back onto West Brook Road. Continue on West Brook. You'll pass Kitchell Lake on your right. Immediately after the lake is Morsetown Road. Make a right on Morsetown.

Be prepared for some hill climbing as Morsetown Road winds through the heart of West Milford Township. Up the road a bit you'll pass Carpi Lake on your left and some scattered residential areas. Although Morsetown Road has no real shoulders, it is not a major road and traffic is usually light.

Continue on Morsetown Road to the "T" intersection. Here Morsetown runs into Marshall Hill Road. Make a right and follow Marshall Hill to Greenwood Lake Turnpike. At the fork, bear right. Shortly thereafter, Marshall Hill Road becomes Greenwood Lake Turnpike, also known as Route 511.

You'll remain on Greenwood Lake Turnpike until the intersection with Skyline Drive and the return to Ringwood Plaza, some seven miles later. You'll pass a portion of the Wanaque Wildlife Management Area and cross over the Wanaque River which connects the Wanaque Reservoir and Greenwood Lake.

You'll also encounter a couple of fork-intersections. Bear right at both of them and follow Route 511 signs. This is a major road; some sections of it have shoulders, but most don't. Fortunately the road is wide and you're able to stay out of the way of cars. Ride with caution, nonetheless. The speed limit on Greenwood Lake Turnpike (Route 511) is fifty miles per hour.

Eventually you'll come to a long stretch of Greenwood Lake Turnpike that hugs the northern section of the Wanaque Reservoir. Enjoy the view of the clear, blue water and the tiny islands that dot the basin.

Greenwood Lake Turnpike will gradually bend around the reservoir. The road should be familiar to those cyclists who have ridden the Ringwood Roundabout tour, once they are on the eastern shore of the Wanaque Reservoir. There is an "island" at the base of Skyline Drive with flagpoles bearing the American and state of New Jersey flags.

Turn left here onto Skyline Drive, and ride up the steep hill back to Ringwood Plaza where the tour ends.

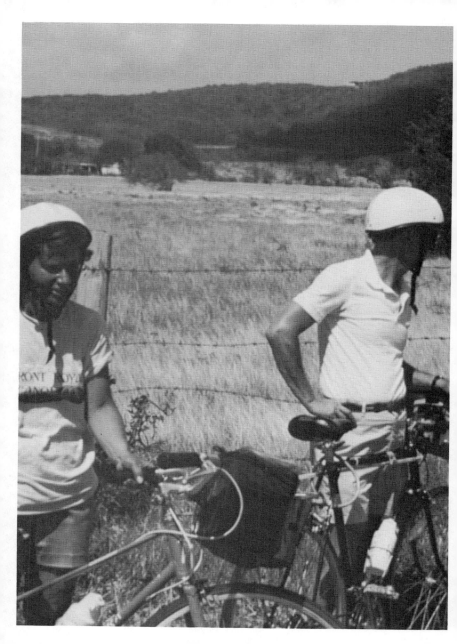

3. Swartzwood Lake Loop

County: Sussex
Number of Miles: 12
Degree of Difficulty: Moderate
Terrain: Some hills
Surface: Good
Things to See: Villages of Stillwater and Middleville, Robbins
General Store, Swartzwood Lake, Swartzwood Lake State
Park

Swartzwood Lake is a popular Northwest New Jersey destination
for bathers and boaters. Swartzwood Lake State Park isn't a large
park—the lake is surely the main attraction—but the bicycle ride to
and through the park is indeed worthwhile. And when the weather
is hot there is always the opportunity for a cool dip in the lake.

The tour begins in the village of Stillwater at the intersection
of routes 521 and 610. Proceed up Route 521 North toward the
village of Middleville. Route 521 isn't a heavy traffic road, but
cars will certainly pass you often enough to warrant riding with
caution. Be prepared, too, for a few climbs and descents, although no hill that you'll encounter is particularly challenging.

About three miles up the road at the Middleville Inn, you'll see a
sign for Route 521, Swartzwood, and Branchville. Make a right. Immediately thereafter you'll come to Robbins General Store, a delightful place to stop for a snack or drink. Notice that the store is also
Middleville's post office and has Middleville's one and only gas pump.

Continue along Route 521 North. About a mile after leaving
Middleville you'll come to your first glance of Swartzwood Lake on
your right. What you'll see, however, is only a small, skinny finger of
Swartzwood. The lake gets bigger and wider up ahead.

Proceed on Route 521 North to the intersection with Route
622, also known as Swartzwood Road. You'll see a sign for
Swartzwood State Park, too. Make a right here. A half mile down
Route 622, you'll enter into Swartzwood Lake State Park property.

Little
Swartzwood
Lake

SWARTZWOOD RD.
RTE #622

Swartzwood
State Park

SWARTZWOOD EAST

Swartzwood
Lake

RTE #521

SHORE RD.

RTE #619

N

STILLWATER RD.
RTE #521

FREDON RD.
RTE #610

START
STOP

How To Get There: Route 80, Exit 12, to Route 521 North. Route 521 North to the village of Stillwater.

SWARTZWOOD LAKE LOOP: DIRECTIONS AT A GLANCE

1. Route 521 North to Middleville Inn. Make right. (You're still on Route 521, however.)
2. Right onto Route 622.
3. Right onto Route 619.
4. Right onto Route 610.
5. Follow Route 610 to Route 610-Route 521 intersection, the tour's starting and stopping point.

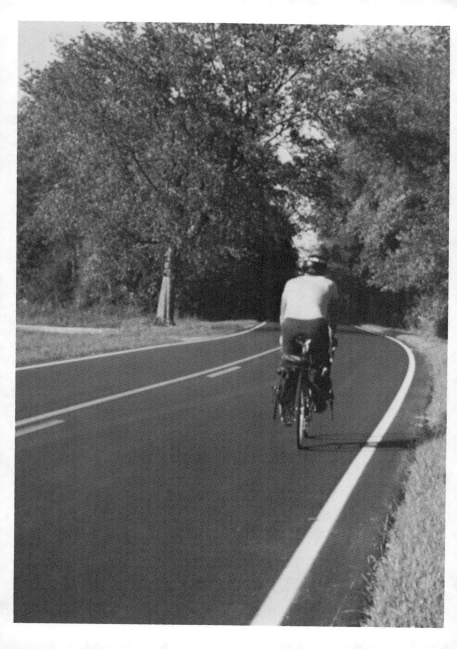

Proceed on Route 622 until the intersection with Route 619. Make a right here. (Route 619 is also known as Swartzwood East Shore Road and once you leave the park, East Shore Drive. It's easiest to follow signs for Route 619.)

Approximately a half mile down Route 619 you'll come to the formal entrance of Swartzwood State Park on your right. Pull into the park if only to get a good glimpse of Swartzwood Lake. You can purchase food and drinks here, or, as already mentioned, you can go swimming. Some cyclists might opt for a picnic lunch and a swim—a great idea if you want to make this tour an all-day activity.

Afterwards, leave Swartzwood Lake State Park the same way you came in and make a right back onto Route 619. Proceed on Route 619 to the fork intersection with Route 610, some five miles south of the Swartzwood Lake State Park entrance/exit. Bear right. A hundred yards later you'll come to a stop sign. Bear right again. You'll now be on Route 610.

Follow Route 610 back into Stillwater. Along the way you'll pass some picturesque horse farms and ride over a single lane bridge. You'll then enter the village of Stillwater and pass the Inn at Stillwater, a couple of antique shops, and Tarriss's General Store. All of this is just a hundred yards or so from the Route 610-Route 521 intersection, the starting point of the tour.

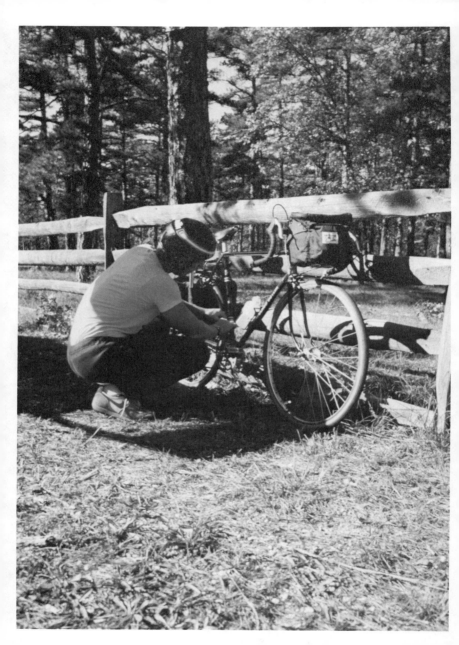

4. Delaware Water Gap

County: Sussex
Number of Miles: 11.4
Degree of Difficulty: Moderate to difficult
Terrain: Some hills
Surface: Good
Things to See: Delaware Water Gap National Recreation Area,
Delaware River, Walpack Wildlife Management Area

Sometimes it is difficult to believe that the Delaware Water Gap National Recreation Area is actually a part of New Jersey. The bold mountain landscapes; the cool, crisp air; the thick forests; and the abundant wildlife make the Delaware Water Gap seem far removed from New Jersey's urban bustle and suburbs. And yet they're little more than an hour away. Along with Southern New Jersey's Pine Barrens (see Pine Barrens tour), the Water Gap is a treasure trove of unspoiled natural beauty. And like the Pine Barrens, it's a great place to cycle.

But what about all the ridges and steep inclines, you ask? Just how rewarding can climbing the Kittatinny Mountain Range on a bicycle be? Have no fear. Where there are rivers, there are usually valleys and some pretty good flatland. And where there is flatland in a mountainous region, there is probably a road. Such is the case here.

Actually, getting to the Delaware Water Gap tour starting point by car is considerably more challenging than riding it by bike. Although there are a couple of good bike climbs, none are so demanding that the tour should be judged "difficult." One section of the tour follows the Delaware River. Another section follows the Flat Brook. Both make for pleasurable riding.

It is a good idea to make certain you have adequate water, tools, and whatever snacks you might want to munch on along the way before you start out. There are no stores and few houses on the route. Traffic will probably be light, except on summer weekends. The roads are patrolled by park rangers, and there is a ranger station farther north on Route 615. Thus, if an emergency should occur, help isn't too far away.

29

Old Mine Road

Pompey Rd.

Walpack-Flatbrook Rte. #615

Water Gap National Recreation Area

Old Mine Rd.

Walpack Wildlife Management Area

Delaware River

Pennsylvania

Rte. #615

N

Delaware River

Perry Rd.

Old Mine Rd.

Start

Old Mine Road

Flatbrookville – Stillwater Rd.

Rte. #615

How To Get There: Route 80, Exit 12, to Route 521 North. Route 521 North to Route 617. Route 617 to Route 624. Route 624 to Flatbrookville-Stillwater Road. Flatbrookville-Stillwater Road to Old Mine Road. Old Mine Road to intersection with Route 615 (Walpack-Flatbrook Road).

DELAWARE WATER GAP: DIRECTIONS AT A GLANCE

1. Left at the stop sign where Route 615 and Old Mine Road merge.
2. Proceed on Route 615/Old Mine Road.
3. Right at the fork onto Pompey Road.
4. Right back onto Route 615.
5. Route 615 to starting/stopping point.

The tour begins at the merge of Old Mine Road and Route 615 (Walpack-Flatbrook Road). Park your car in the small parking area on the side of the Old Mine Road Bridge that's usually reserved for fishermen. Facing the stop sign at the Old Mine Road-Route 615 merge, make a left and ride south on Route 615/Old Mine Road. Ride with caution; the road has no shoulders.

A mile from your starting point, you'll pass a historic marker on the opposite side of the road. It gives a brief account of the historical importance of Old Mine Road, which allegedly was cleared and opened for travel around 1650. This would make it the oldest road still in use in the United States.

After you round the bend on Route 615/Old Mine Road, you'll begin to catch glimpses of the Delaware River on your left. Across it is Pennsylvania. As you continue north on Old Mine Road, you'll see cars parked on the sides of the road. Often these are the vehicles of bird watchers and hikers, but during hunting season they are almost always the cars of hunters. The pops you'll undoubtedly hear off in the distance are the sounds of hunters' guns.

About five miles or so from the Old Mine Road historic marker, you'll come to a fork in the road. To your left is Old Mine Road. To your right is Pompey Road. Take the latter. North of this intersection, Old Mine Road is not in good shape generally. Besides, Pompey Road offers the only Water Gap loop connection to your starting point.

Pompey Road is the steepest climb you'll encounter on this tour. At the end of it approximately two miles away, you'll come to a stop sign and the Route 615 intersection. Make a right and head south on Route 615, also known in this section as Walpack-Flatbrook Road. Soon you'll enter the Walpack Wildlife Management Area. On your left is the Flat Brook.

Continue south on Route 615 to the Old Mine Road bridge, your starting and ending point. In the fall this area is ablaze with color. Be advised though that the leaves fall off the trees earlier here than in other sections of the state. If you plan your ride sometime during the foliage spectacle, the best time to go is late September or early October.

5. Old Mine Road Run

County: Warren
Number of Miles: 24
Degree of Difficulty: Moderate
Terrain: Mostly flat
Surface: Mostly good
Things to See: Delaware Water Gap National Recreation Area, Delaware Water Gap Visitor's Center, Delaware River, Old Mine Road, Millbrook Village

The Old Mine Road Run is a sister tour of the Delaware Water Gap tour. Both are located in the Delaware Water Gap National Recreation Area. Both are particularly scenic rides along the Delaware River. But where the Delaware Water Gap tour is a loop tour that begins and ends at the same point without riding on any road twice, the Old Mine Road Run is a "backtrack" tour. In other words, cyclists will ride up Old Mine Road from the Delaware Water Gap Visitor's Center to Millbrook Village, a restored, century-old Water Gap community. Then they will turn around and return to the Visitor's Center, once again, by way of Old Mine Road.

There is no other way to enjoy the scenery of Old Mine Road and end up where you started. Roads are scarce in the Water Gap Recreation Area. Those alternative roads, which a touring cyclist might consider as a way to avoid backtracking on Old Mine Road, are not always maintained or else go in the wrong direction. Any attempt at riding on these roads would require more time and a fat-tire mountain bike. The tour would also add up to much more than twenty-four miles.

There is really no disadvantage to riding up and down Old Mine Road. It is one of the prettiest stretches of road in all New Jersey. Although you share the road with automobiles, bicycle traffic is common on Old Mine Road, especially on weekends in spring, summer, and fall.

As mentioned in the Delaware Water Gap tour, travelers supposedly began using Old Mine Road as early as 1650. Dutch settlers in New Jersey and New York used it to haul copper ore from the

How To Get There: Route 80 West, Exit 1, to Delaware Water Gap National Recreation Area Visitor's Center.

OLD MINE ROAD RUN: DIRECTIONS AT A GLANCE

1. Delaware Water Gap Visitor's Center parking lot to Old Mine Road.
2. Old Mine Road to Millbrook Village.
3. Old Mine Road back to Delaware Water Gap Visitor's Center.

Pahaquarry Mines in New Jersey to what is today Kingston, New York. The Old Mine Road is said to be the oldest road in America still in use. Its length is more than a hundred miles.

Leave your car in the parking lot of the Delaware Water Gap Visitor's Center just off the western end (or beginning) of Route 80. Inside the Visitor's Center are free brochures and maps of the Recreation Area and a few small displays that explain the geological origins of the Delaware Water Gap millions of years ago. Rangers stationed at the Visitor's Center will answer any questions you might have about the Recreation Area.

Like the Delaware Water Gap tour described earlier, the Old Mine Road Run is without stores or places to stop and eat. Bring what you want to snack on or drink with you. Also, make certain you take the proper tools and spare parts (see the bicycle touring information in the beginning of the book) with you in case a breakdown or tire puncture should occur. If there is an emergency, however, there are enough cars traveling on Old Mine Road so it would not be impossible to flag one down. Also, park rangers patrol Old Mine Road on a routine basis.

Ride out of the Visitor's Center parking lot and onto Old Mine Road. Not far from the Visitor's Center you'll come to, of all things, a traffic light. It's there because this section of Old Mine Road isn't wide enough for two cars to pass at the same time. A red light for you means a green light for cars heading to the Visitor's Center and Route 80. Although the signal is somewhat long (at least 3 minutes), adhere to it. Approaching motorists don't expect bicyclists in their path when their light is green, and they take up virtually all of the road. By being impatient, you could cause a serious accident.

Continue riding north on Old Mine Road. Admire the beautiful river scenes to your left. You'll pass through Worthington State Forest and ride by a couple of picnic areas and campgrounds. You'll do a little climbing, but certainly nothing that will cause you much sweat.

It is twelve miles from the Visitor's Center to the restored village of Millbrook. Here, volunteers dress up the way Water Gap settlers did more than a hundred years ago. Lock up your bike and tour the village. Your first stop should be the Spangenberg Cabin where you can view a short slide show that tells the story of

Millbrook. You can also pick up a self-guided tour brochure that is most helpful as you walk around Millbrook. After Spangenberg Cabin, visit the Trauger House, the blacksmith shop, the general store, the grist mill, and the other restored buildings of Millbrook. This is a fine place to have a picnic and rest up for your ride back to the Visitor's Center, too.

After your tour of Millbrook, begin the ride back to the Visitor's Center. There are no turns or specific directions other than to follow Old Mine Road to its end.

6. Jockey Hollow

County: Morris
Number of Miles: 3.8
Degree of Difficulty: Easy
Terrain: Some hills
Surface: Good
Things to See: Jockey Hollow section of Morristown National
   Historic Park, Visitor's Center, Wick Farmhouse, Pennsylvania
   Line, Grand Parade, Guerin House

The tour of Jockey Hollow is the shortest of all the tours in this book. Since it is also on roads in Morristown National Historic Park, it is, in many ways, the ideal family tour. Kids aged ten and up can enjoy this tour without worry of overly strenuous climbs, rough road surfaces, high mileage, or fast moving traffic. (The roads in the park are not traffic-free, but the speed limit in most parts is twenty-five miles per hour.)

There is also much to see and do at Jockey Hollow. It was here in 1777 and then again in 1779–80 that General George Washington and his troops spent the winter resting and then training and preparing to fight the British in the spring.

The winter of 1777 was better than the one of 1779–80. In early 1777 Washington and the Continental Army settled down for the winter after the two important victories at Trenton and Princeton. (See Washington Crossing tour.) It wasn't a particularly harsh winter, and by spring, Washington's army was sufficiently rested and replenished and ready to fight again.

The winter of 1779-80 was, however, another story. It was a severe four months, from December through March, and the army suffered. There were heavy snowstorms and bitter cold nights. Food and supplies were scarce. A smallpox epidemic broke out. Some said it was the worst winter of the eighteenth century. Yet, somehow the Continental Army endured at Jockey Hollow, the main encampment. How the army survived is what Morristown National Historic Park is all about.

Lewis Morris Cty Park Entrance

Grand Parade

Pa. Line

Parking

TOUR RD.

JOCKEY HOLLOW RD.

Wick Farm

Visitor Ctr.

START STOP

Parking

N

How To Get There: Route 287 to Tempe Wick Road to entrance of Jockey Hollow section of Morristown National Historic Park.

JOCKEY HOLLOW: DIRECTIONS AT A GLANCE

1. Leave Visitor's Center parking lot and proceed up Tour Road.
2. Bear left at Pennsylvania Line/Grand Parade intersection.
3. Bear right at Lewis Morris County Park entrance.
4. Right at stop sign onto Jockey Hollow Road.
5. Jockey Hollow Road to Visitor's Center parking lot.

Before beginning your ride, spend some time at the Jockey Hollow Visitor's Center. Here you'll be able to view a thirteen-minute movie that details the hardships of daily existence at Jockey Hollow in 1779-80. In addition, there are exhibits and displays of artifacts found at Jockey Hollow. A park ranger will answer your questions about that famous winter and events in the park as well as the historical importance of Jockey Hollow. Free maps and brochures are available. Books and souvenirs are for sale.

After visiting the Visitor's Center, use the rear exit and walk to the Wick Farm, a few hundred feet away. This was the headquarters of General Arthur St. Clair. It was also one of the few comfortable buildings to reside in at Jockey Hollow in 1779-80.

Make your way back to the Visitor's Center parking lot where the tour of Jockey Hollow begins. As you can see from the map, the tour is simply a small loop that begins and ends in this parking lot.

Proceed up Tour Road, the road to the left of the Visitor's Center. A mile or so up the road you'll come to an intersection. If you go right on Tour Road, you'll take the abbreviated tour of Jockey Hollow, which adds up to a mere two miles. Instead, stay left and ride into the parking area. Lock your bike and leave it here, and walk up to the Pennsylvania Line and Grand Parade grounds on the hill opposite this parking lot.

The hill is called Sugar Loaf Hill. The huts on top of it are similar to those that two thousand soldiers of the First and Second Pennsylvania Brigades called home. Behind the huts are the Grand Parade grounds. Here soldiers marched, drilled, and trained.

Return to the parking area and your bike. Ride out the exit, make a left, and head toward Lewis Morris County Park. You'll soon come to the entrance of the park. Those who wish to add a few miles to this tour can explore the roads and scenery of the park. However, be advised that there are hills, some steep. There is also no loop road that will bring you back to this entrance/exit.

Continue on the park road to the stop sign at the next intersection. Make a right here onto Jockey Hollow Road and follow signs to the Visitor's Center. Immediately after making the right, you'll come to the Guerin House, home of a Jockey Hollow blacksmith and his family during the encampment. At this point you'll have to go up and down some hills, but the scenery and sense of history that surrounds you makes the effort worthwhile.

About three quarters of a mile from the Guerin House you'll come to a circular building. Here you'll find restrooms and a map of the area. The road beyond is dotted with historical markers, including one that tells of the Old Camp Road and another that highlights the story of the Maryland Brigade at Jockey Hollow.

Continue on Jockey Hollow Road back to the Visitor's Center where the tour concludes.

Note: There is more to see and experience in Morristown National Historical Park. On the way to the city of Morristown, just a few miles away, is Fort Nonsense. It was here that Washington had his troops dig trenches and build embankments to keep them occupied during the winter. Hence the name, "Nonsense."

In Morristown, you can visit Washington's Headquarters at the Ford Mansion. Here military strategy and day-to-day plans for the troops were worked out. There is also a museum here.

I didn't include these two points of interest in the tour for two reasons. The first is that to get to them requires leaving park grounds and riding on fairly busy roads. The second is because I wanted to include a "short" tour in a setting where there was much to see and do and that could be enjoyed as a fun family ride.

The Jockey Hollow loop tour fulfills this aim nicely. More experienced riders might want to ride up Western Avenue to Fort Nonsense and then on to Washington's Headquarters on Morris Avenue, however.

7. Great Swamp Swing

County: Morris
Number of Miles: 16.6
Degree of Difficulty: Moderate
Terrain: Some hills
Surface: Good
Things to See: Village of New Vernon, Morris County Outdoor Education Center, Great Swamp Natural Wildlife Refuge, Wildlife Observation Center

The Great Swamp Natural Wildlife Refuge is a delicate ecological preserve nestled in the southeast corner of Morris County. It's the end result of a huge glacial lake that once covered areas of Morris and Somerset Counties more than 15,000 years ago.

Back in 1960, the Great Swamp almost became a fourth New York-New Jersey metropolitan area airport. But environmentalists and concerned citizens fought to save the Great Swamp and won. Today the Great Swamp is under jurisdiction of the Department of the Interior. The 6,800-acre tract is the home of many wildlife and plant species as well as the resting place for migrating waterfowl.

The Great Swamp Swing tour is actually part of a larger tour put out in brochure form by the Bicycle Advocate's office of the New Jersey Department of Transportation. The tour of the Great Swamp consists of two loops. What follows is Loop #1.

The Great Swamp Swing begins in the village of New Vernon. Those arriving by car should look for parking near New Vernon's post office and small cluster of stores. Begin the tour by riding east (opposite the direction you came) on Village Road. You can expect some traffic on the road. Although it has no shoulder area, Village Road is wide enough so you won't have to compete with vehicles for your share of it. There is ample room for you to ride alongside traffic.

Continue on Village Road. You'll pass a connection with Pleasantville Road. Make a right at the stop sign onto Spring Valley Road. Spring Valley turns into Green Village Road. Follow Green Village Road to Hickory Place, a shortcut and alternative to dealing with the Shunpike Road/Southern Boulevard intersection a few hundred feet away at the stop sign.

HICKORY PL.

SOUTHERN BLVD.

SPRING VALLEY/ GREEN VILLAGE RD.

FAIRMOUNT AVE.

VILLAGE RD.

LEE'S HILL RD.

START/ STOP

Great Swamp Ntl. Wildlife Refuge

LONG HILL RD.

MEYERSVILLE RD.

NEW VERNON RD.

N

How To Get There: Route 287 to Glen Alpin Road in Harding Township. Glen Alpin eventually turns into Village Road. Village Road to the post office in New Vernon.

GREAT SWAMP SWING: DIRECTIONS AT A GLANCE

1. Village Road to Spring Valley Road.
2. Right onto Spring Valley-Green Village Road.
3. Right onto Hickory Place.
4. Right onto Southern Boulevard.
5. Right onto Fairmount Avenue.
6. Right onto Meyersville Road.
7. Right onto New Vernon Road which turns into Long Hill Road.
8. Right onto Lee's Hill Road.
9. Right onto Village Road.

Make a right onto Hickory Place and then another right onto a less hectic part of Southern Boulevard. Since Southern Boulevard winds across the boroughs of Madison and Chatham, you'll pass through a few residential areas. The Great Swamp Natural Wildlife Refuge is on your right, however.

Eventually you'll come to the Morris County Great Swamp Outdoor Center. A stop at the center is recommended if you're interested in the ecology of the Great Swamp. At the center you can view wildlife and natural history displays and special exhibits that deal with the formation of the swamp.

The only problem concerning the Outdoor Center for bicyclists is getting there. The driveway off Southern Boulevard that leads to the Outdoor Center is rough and rocky. You'd be wise to walk your bike to the Center to safeguard against getting a flat tire.

After your visit to the Outdoor Center, return to Southern Boulevard. Turn right onto the boulevard and ride to the traffic light and intersection with Fairmount Avenue. Make a right and proceed down Fairmount to the intersection with Meyersville Road about a mile away.

Make a right onto Meyersville Road. Continue on it until you come to the intersection with New Vernon Road. Make a right on New Vernon and ride into the Great Swamp Natural Wildlife Refuge. A mile or so from the beginning of New Vernon Road, you'll come to the Wildlife Observation Center where there are nature trails, which lead further into the heart of the Great Swamp. There is even a bike stand where you can lock your bike while hiking the trail.

Farther along New Vernon you'll come across more scenic views of the Great Swamp landscape. Depending on the season you might also spot migratory birds resting or feeding. New Vernon Road will turn into Long Hill Road once you leave the Great Swamp refuge. Proceed on Long Hill to the intersection with Lee's Hill Road, sometimes referred to as Logansville Road. Make a right. A quarter mile up on Lee's Hill Road will be the intersection with Village Road. Turn right here and proceed back into New Vernon where the tour began.

8. Tour of Tewksbury

County: Hunterdon
Number of Miles: 17.7
Degree of Difficulty: Moderate to difficult
Terrain: Hills, some steep
Surface: Good
Things to See: Village of Oldwick, Oldwick General Store,
    Village of Mountainville, Mountainville General Store,
    Hunterdon County farm area

This tour is one of my favorites, especially in the fall when the trees of the Tewksbury section of Hunterdon County are a carnival of color. You'll ride on some of the prettiest country lanes in the state—stop at a general store for some fresh morning coffee—and you'll wonder why, in the past, you traveled all the way to Vermont and New Hampshire to admire their classic country landscapes when equally touching ones were right here in New Jersey.

The tour commences in Oldwick, a picturesque old village of antique shops and restored country homes. First settled in the mid-eighteenth century, Oldwick was originally known as New Germantown.

Begin your ride on King's Street, the road between the Oldwick General Store and the Tewksbury Inn, a popular restaurant and drinking establishment. Proceed out of Oldwick on King's Street. Not far from the Oldwick General Store, you'll find yourself out in the country. Don't be surprised if you spot a deer or two on your ride. The Oldwick area supports a healthy deer population.

Some two miles from Oldwick you'll come to a single-lane bridge. Proceed over it with caution. Just beyond the bridge is a stop sign and intersection. Make a right here on Rockaway Road. At the fork in the road a short distance away, bear to your right and continue on Rockaway Road. You will pass over two more single-lane bridges.

At the "T" intersection and the corner of Rockaway Road and Water Street, you will come to the Mountainville General Store. If you're ready for something to drink or a bite to eat, this is a good

COKESBURY / FAIRMOUNT RD.
(RTE #512)

COKESBURY RD.

GUINEA-HOLLOW RD.

COKESBURY RD. / DAVIS RD.

Mountainville General Store

WATER STREET

ROCKAWAY RD.

HILL AND DALE RD.

Oldwick General Store

OLD TURNPIKE RD.

BISSELL RD.

KING'S ST.

START STOP

Tewksbury Inn

RTE # 523 OLDWICK RD.

N

How To Get There: Route 22 to Route 523 North (Oldwick Road) to village of Oldwick.

TOUR OF TEWKSBURY: DIRECTIONS AT A GLANCE

1. King's Street to Rockaway Road.
2. Right onto Rockaway Road.
3. Right at Water Street intersection.
4. Left onto Guinea-Hollow Road.
5. Left onto Fairmount Road.
6. Left onto Cokesbury Road.
7. Bear right at fork (stay on Cokesbury Road).
8. Pass through two stop signs; bear left at the first one and make a right at the second one, remaining on Cokesbury Road.
9. Left onto Bissell Road.
10. Left onto Rockaway Road.
11. Right onto Hill and Dale Road.
12. Right onto Old Turnpike Road.

place for it. If you're not, make a right at the "T" intersection. (It's a left if you crossed the intersection into the Moutainville General Store parking lot.)

Just on the outskirts of Mountainville is another single-lane bridge. Immediately after the bridge, make a left onto Guinea–Hollow Road. Proceed on Guinea-Hollow to the stop sign and "T" intersection. Make a left here onto Fairmount Road, also known as Route 512. Follow Fairmount to Cokesbury Road on the outskirts of the tiny town of Califon and make a left.

Be prepared for a steep climb up Cokesbury Road. At the top of the hill, you'll come to a fork in the road. Bear right onto Davis Road/Cokesbury Road. (There may not be any street signs here.) Follow this road to another fork; again bear to your right, which means you'll remain on Davis Road/Cokesbury Road. Much of this section of the tour is downhill, although there will be a couple of slight inclines.

At the bottom of the hill, you'll come to a stop sign. Bear left. Shortly thereafter is another stop sign and intersection. This links Cokesbury Road and Water Street. Make a right and continue down Cokesbury Road to Bissell Road where you'll make a left. On the way, you'll pass an old Methodist church and cemetery.

Proceed on Bissell Road. It's a winding country road with farms on both sides. Bear right at the Bissell Road–Still Hollow Road intersection, and continue on Bissell Road until its intersection with Rockaway Road a couple of miles later. Make a left on Rockaway Road.

If this stretch of road looks familiar, it's because you rode on it earlier on your way to Mountainville. You won't be on it long, however. Make a right onto Hill and Dale Road that is about a half mile away. Hill and Dale Road cuts through prime Hunterdon County farming area.

At the stop sign and intersection, make a right onto Old Turnpike Road, which in Oldwick becomes Oldwick Road. Old Turnpike Road is a fairly busy road for these parts since it eventually connects with Route 22. If you approached Oldwick and the start of this tour by car from Route 22, you took Route 523 to the Oldwick General Store.

Follow Old Turnpike Road into the village of Oldwick and the Oldwick General Store. The tour ends here.

9. Round Valley Ramble

County: Hunterdon
Number of Miles: 17.4
Degree of Difficulty: Moderate
Terrain: Hills
Surface: Good
Things to See: Village of Lebanon, Round Valley Recreation
Area, Stanton General Store

Round Valley Recreation Area is made up of a huge, almost oval reservoir and over 4,000 acres of park land in the middle of Hunterdon County. There are plenty of outdoor activities to be enjoyed here: wilderness camping, swimming, picnicking, boating, fishing, hiking and scuba diving. But even though Round Valley doesn't have much in the way of bicycle paths or loops, the area and roads surrounding the reservoir more than make up for this deficiency.

The tour begins at the intersection of Main and Cherry Streets in the village of Lebanon. Find a parking space along either of these streets. Proceed toward Round Valley by way of Cherry Street, which will take you out of Lebanon and into the countryside. Eventually, Cherry Street will turn into Route 629 (also known as Lebanon-Stanton Road). Once you reach Round Valley, you'll have a wonderful view of the reservoir and encompassing woodland.

At the stop sign make a left; you'll still be on Route 629. On weekends this part of Route 629 can get busy, since it leads to the main entrance of Round Valley. Fortunately, there is adequate shoulder space to cycle on and stay out of any traffic you might encounter.

Proceed down Route 629 until you come to the entrance of the Round Valley Recreation Area. Make a left into the park and ride to the Visitor's Center. Unlike other state park visitor's centers, the one at Round Valley has little in the way of exhibits or displays. However, you can pick up information on park activities and any special events going on as well as a map should you wish to do a bit of cycling in the park before continuing with the remainder of

How To Get There: Route 22 to Main Street in Lebanon.

ROUND VALLEY RAMBLE: DIRECTIONS AT A GLANCE

1. Cherry Street to Route 629.
2. Left at stop sign (still on Route 629).
3. Left into entrance of Round Valley Recreation Area.
4. Left onto Route 629.
5. Left onto Stanton Mountain Road.
6. Right onto Dreahook Road.
7. Left onto Route 523.
8. Left onto Mountain Road.
9. Left onto Railroad Avenue.
10. Left onto Old Mountain Road.
11. Right onto Cherry Street.

this tour. You can ride to the swimming and picnic areas and then turn around and come back to the Visitor's Center where you'll follow the road to the entrance/exit of the park.

Make a left at the exit and continue on Route 629. You'll pass through scenic Hunterdon County countryside. You'll also pass through new residential areas dotted with high-priced homes where once were working farms.

About six miles from the entrance to Round Valley Recreation Area, you'll come to the Stanton General Store. The General Store is one of only three public buildings in the tiny village of Stanton. The other two are the post office and church, and you'll pass both of them, too. But first, stop at the General Store for a snack and something to drink.

Exit the General Store parking area onto Stanton Mountain Road. *Note:* You might recall that you passed an earlier entrance onto Stanton Mountain Road. That's because the road forms a half-loop as it winds over Stanton Mountain (see map). A half mile or so later you'll make a right onto Dreahook Road. Continue on Dreahook, passing Round Valley Road and another residential area until you come to the "T" intersection. There is a stop sign here. Make a left onto Route 523 (Flemington-Whitehouse Road). A mile and a half from the Dreahook-Route 523 intersection, make a left onto Mountain Road. Ride to the second single-lane bridge. Immediately after the bridge, make a left onto Railroad Avenue. Railroad Avenue turns into Old Mountain Road after the Deer Path intersection. Make a left at this intersection and cross over the railroad tracks.

Proceed along Old Mountain Road. Round Valley is on your left. Approximately three miles from where you crossed the railroad tracks, you'll come to another intersection. Make a right here, onto Cherry Street, and ride back to Lebanon where the tour concludes.

10. Flemington Flow

County: Hunterdon
Number of Miles: 9
Degree of Difficulty: Easy
Terrain: Mostly flat
Surface: Fair
Things to See: Town of Flemington and its numerous historic
buildings and shopping outlets; Hunterdon countryside

Over the past twenty years Flemington has become more than the county seat of Hunterdon and Western New Jersey's agriculture center. Once entrepreneurs realized the commercial potential of Flemington's Main Street with its many nineteenth-century buildings and classic small-town setting, Flemington quickly became a tourist and shopping attraction. Today, the town is bursting with outlet stores and boutiques that attract visitors from all over the New York-New Jersey metropolitan area.

There are other things to do in Flemington besides spend money, however. You can watch the glass cutters at work in the Flemington Cut Glass Company on Main Street. The County Courthouse, also on Main Street, was the site of the famous Lindbergh Trial in 1935 which attracted international attention. Bruno Hauptmann was convicted of the kidnapping and murder of the son of aviator Charles Lindbergh. Hauptmann was sentenced to death and later executed for his crimes.

You can also visit the Doric House (Maple Avenue and Main Street), home of the Hunterdon County Historical Society. Inside the house is a small museum. The Fleming Castle (Bonnell Street) once was an old stagecoach depot and inn. The Daughters of the American Revolution conduct tours of Fleming Castle, but only by appointment. (Call 908–782–4655.)

It is possible to bicycle through the sidestreets of Flemington and admire the town's many historic buildings, but this tour begins on the edge of Main Street's shopping area and continues through the countryside on the outskirts of town.

N

How To Get There: Route 202 to Church Street in Flemington. Right on Main Street. Main Street to Presbyterian Church on East Main Street.

FLEMINGTON FLOW: DIRECTIONS AT A GLANCE

1. Left out Presbyterian Church parking lot.
2. Cross over Route 31. Proceed on Route 523.
3. Left at intersection. Continue on Route 523.
4. Right at "T" intersection (still Route 523).
5. Right onto Barley Sheaf Road.
6. Right onto Rockafellow Mill Road.
7. Right at intersection immediately after Raritan River bridge.
8. River Road to Pennsylvania Avenue.
9. Pennsylvania Avenue to Route 31. Cross Route 31.
10. Pennsylvania Avenue to East Main Street.
11. Right on East Main Street.
12. Left back into Presbyterian Church parking lot.

The tour begins in the parking lot of the Flemington Presbyterian Church on East Main Street. Ride out the driveway and proceed down East Main Street, away from the center of Flemington. A half mile later you'll come to the Route 31 intersection and traffic light. Cross over Route 31. You will now be on Route 523. Follow Route 523 (Flemington-Junction Road). Admittedly, this part of the tour isn't very scenic. The area is a combination of old and new Flemington and reveals the industry that has settled here.

At the stop sign, make a left. You are still on Route 523. At the "T" intersection and stop sign, make a right. You're still on Route 523. (If you turned left, you would be on Route 612.) Pass the Lipton Tea Company plant on your right and cross over the Raritan River. Follow Route 523 to Barley Sheaf Road where you'll make a right. The scenery improves considerably in this section of the tour. Years ago this was all farmland. Today development has occurred here, but not enough to destroy the largely agricultural setting that Hunterdon County is known for.

Make a right onto Rockafellow Mill Road. You'll cross over two sets of railroad tracks and re-cross the Raritan River. As you cross the bridge, look to your right at the small waterfall. Make a right at the intersection immediately after the bridge onto River Road, and you'll be riding parallel to the Raritan River.

Up ahead not quite a mile, you'll come to Pennsylvania Avenue. Proceed on Pennsylvania Avenue. Your next intersection will be one with Route 31. Cross over Route 31. You're still on Pennsylvania Avenue. Take Pennsylvania Avenue to East Main Street where the tour began. East Main Street is the second stop sign on Pennsylvania Avenue. Make a right onto East Main Street and a left back into the Presbyterian Church parking lot. This ends the tour.

Note: This tour is courtesy of the Hunterdon County Park System. It is number 9 of the series of tours it publishes for bicyclists who wish to explore in depth the back roads of Hunterdon, arguably the state's best county for bicyling.

11. Stockton—Covered Bridge Tour

County: Hunterdon
Number of Miles: 19.4
Degree of Difficulty: Moderate
Terrain: Hills, some steep
Surface: Good
Things to See: Stockton, Hunterdon County farmland, Covered
   Bridge, Rosemont General Store, Delaware & Raritan Canal,
   Delaware River

Stockton is a little hamlet nestled on the banks of the Delaware River, just a couple of miles north of Lambertville's shopping district. Many of the homes found in Stockton date back 150 years or more, and there is a cheery warmth to the town that reminds one of New England, especially Vermont.

Those who already know Stockton probably do so because of Colligan's Stockton Inn, a popular bed & breakfast-styled inn, which also includes two superb restaurants, Colligan's and The Fox. Established in the early eighteenth century, the inn was made somewhat famous in this century when Richard Rodgers, of the great American songwriting team of Rodgers and Hart, wrote his song "There's a Small Hotel with a Wishing Well" while visiting Colligan's Stockton Inn. The wishing well Rodgers wrote about is still on the premises, and virtually everyone who eats or stays at the inn throws a penny or two in it for good luck.

This tour begins in Stockton, just across from Colligan's. Colligan's is located on Route 29. However, park your car in front of the small cluster of shops on Bridge Street, Stockton's one and only business area, which faces Colligan's. Notice the bridge two hundred yards away to the west. It connects Stockton with Pennsylvania's Bucks County. Wine lovers should also browse through Phillips', the liquor store on Bridge Street. The selection of wines there is truly outstanding, especially for such a small town as Stockton.

Make a left onto Route 29 North to start this tour, and proceed to the fork in the road not more than a couple hundred yards away.

How To Get There: Route 202 to Route 29. Route 29 to Bridge Street in Stockton.

STOCKTON–COVERED BRIDGE TOUR: DIRECTIONS AT A GLANCE

1. Left onto Route 29.
2. Bear right at fork onto Route 523 (Stockton-Flemington Road).
3. Left onto Rosemont-Ringoes Road (Route 604).
4. Right onto Kingwood-Stockton Road (Route 519).
5. Left onto Route 651 South (Kingwood Byram Road).
6. Left onto Route 29.
7. Bear right at intersection just outside Stockton.
8. Right onto Bridge Street (across from Colligan's Stockton Inn).

Bear right at the fork onto Route 523. The sign at this intersection will indicate that Route 523 is the way to Flemington and Sergeantsville. You'll now pedal up your first hill of this tour, and it's a good one. Near the top you'll see a sign for the Woolverton Inn. This is the second of Stockton's popular bed & breakfast inns. Unlike Colligan's, though, the Woolverton's setting is purely rural.

Proceed on Route 523, which is also called the Stockton-Flemington Road, until the intersection of Route 604. On the way you'll pass working farms, cornfields, picturesque rolling hills, and for many, a view of New Jersey that they thought never existed. If you ever doubted why New Jersey is nicknamed the Garden State, this tour should set aside those doubts.

Make a left onto Route 604, which is also called the Rosemont-Ringoes Road, in the tiny village of Sergeantsville. Sergeantsville was first settled around 1700. It was named for a local Revolutionary War patriot and soldier, Charles Sergeant.

Just down the road on Route 604 you'll come to New Jersey's only remaining covered bridge, the Green-Sergeant Bridge. At one time there were seventy-five covered bridges in the state. This one, built in the early eighteenth century, is now a New Jersey landmark. You'll find a photograph of it in just about every brochure published by New Jersey's Division of Travel and Tourism that relates to Hunterdon County and Jersey's scenic country roads.

Pedal over the covered bridge and continue on the Rosemont-Ringoes Road (Route 604) until the "T" intersection a couple of miles away. Rosemont-Ringoes Road runs into the Kingwood-Stockton Road, also known as Route 519. But before you make a right onto Kingwood-Stockton Road, pay a visit to the Rosemont General Cafe, where a traditional country breakfast awaits you, or at the very least, a cup of freshly brewed coffee. The Rosemont General Cafe can get busy on weekend mornings, especially Sundays. Thus, it is best to arrive early.

Make a right and proceed north on the Kingwood-Stockton Road, once again passing picture perfect country scenes, stone houses over two hundred years old, small farms, and in the fall, the beautiful foliage. Make a left onto Route 651 South (Kingwood Byram Road), a few miles northwest of the Rosemont General Cafe. Continue on Route 651. Eventually you'll come to Route 29 and the Delaware River.

since the Barbertown-Idell Road sign is no more. Later, the Barbertown-Idell Road turns into the Byram-Kingwood Road. Be prepared for more hills. But there is a reward for all your hard pedaling: the last part of the Byram-Kingwood Road (Route 519 Spur), which leads back to Route 29 and the Delaware River, is almost all downhill.

Make a left onto Route 29. Even though Route 29 is a heavily used highway south of Lambertville, since it connects that town with Trenton, this stretch of Route 29 contains much less traffic. And unlike the Lambertville-Trenton section, this section of Route 29 has a smooth, spacious shoulder, ideal for bicycle riding.

You will be able to keep a good, strong pace on Route 29 as you ride back to Stockton. However, those wishing a slower route back to Stockton might opt for riding on the Delaware & Raritan Canal Towpath, which is to your right as you head south on Route 29. You'll see a sign indicating the Delaware & Raritan Canal State Park, Bull's Island Recreation Area soon after the completion of the Kingwood Byram Road and the left onto Route 29. At the sign and entrance to the park, make a right, pick up the towpath, which, by the way, is the same towpath described in the Lambertville Loop, and ride back to Stockton.

Those of you on Route 29 will pass the Prallsville Mills, a renovated 19th-century industrial center worth investigating. After visiting the Prallsville Mills, continue on Route 29 to the intersection outside Stockton. Make a right here and follow signs to Lambertville. An eighth of a mile later, this time at Colligan's Stockton Inn, make a right onto Bridge Street, thus concluding your tour.

12. LAMBERTVILLE LOOP

County: Mercer
Number of Miles: 23
Degree of Difficulty: Moderate to difficult
Terrain: Hills
Surface: Mostly good, but some rough spots
Things to See: Lambertville, Delaware River, Delaware & Raritan
    Canal, Howell Farm, scenic countryside of Mercer County,
    Marshall House, Lambertville House

Lambertville, like its sister town, New Hope, is filled with antique shops and art galleries, cafes and boutiques, restored rowhouses and riverfront recreation. New Hope, located just across the Delaware River in Pennsylvania, is the more popular town, and its distinction of an artist's colony is certainly widespread in the mid-Atlantic region. But, if Lambertville doesn't quite carry the reputation of its counterpart, perhaps that is what makes it more special.

On weekends, Lambertville is less crowded than New Hope and offers less in the way of commercial hype. You can stroll Lambertville's streets without constantly bumping into people. You don't have to wait too long to be seated in its most noted cafes and restaurants during lunch and dinner.

Lambertville is one of the oldest towns in Hunterdon County. Early on it turned to manufacturing as a means of income for its residents. Canning, shoe, and rubber factories dominated the landscape, and its owners hired local men to work them. In 1859 the Lambertville Iron Works opened and continued to operate for almost fifty years.

Today such industries are not part of Lambertville's makeup. But some of the factory buildings have been renovated and turned into clusters of clothing and kitchenware outlet shops, while many of the rowhouses where factory workers lived have been given wonderful facelifts.

It would be a good idea to plan on a full day to complete this tour for two reasons. First, it's a rather long one, with many hills.

How To Get There: Route 202 to Route 29. Route 29 to Bridge Street in Lambertville and the parking lot of the Lambertville Inn.

LAMBERTVILLE LOOP: DIRECTIONS AT A GLANCE

1. Left side of Lambertville Inn—gravel road.
2. Gravel road to Delaware & Raritan Canal Towpath.
3. Left at second bridge over Delaware & Raritan Canal Towpath.
4. Walk up path to Route 29. Cross Route 29 to Valley Road.
5. Valley Road to Woodens Lane and Howell Living History Farm.
6. Left onto Woodens Lane and enter Howell Living Farm.
7. Return back to Woodens Lane after visit to Howell Living History Farm.
8. Left onto Valley Road.
9. Left onto Pleasant Valley Road.
10. Left onto Pleasant Valley-Harbourton Road.
11. Left onto Marshall's Corner Road
12. Left onto Lambertville-Hopewell Turnpike (Route 518).
13. Right onto Rock Road.
14. Left onto Mt. Airy-Harbourton Road (Route 601).
15. Left onto Rocktown-Lambertville Road.
16. Right at conclusion of Rocktown-Lambertville Road.
17. Left at traffic light onto Bridge Street.
18. Bridge Street to Lambertville Inn parking lot.

Second, after you've ridden it, you'll surely want to spend some time in Lambertville browsing through its shops and galleries.

Complete the Lambertville Loop in the morning. You'll ride on the Delaware & Raritan Canal Towpath and back into the nearby Mercer County countryside. (Lambertville is located in Hunterdon County, it's true. But it sits on Hunterdon's southern boundary. For a country lane tour of Hunterdon County, see the Stockton—Covered Bridge Tour.)

After you've completed the tour, have lunch in any of Lambertville's fine eateries. The Inn at the Lambertville Station is highly recommended. Then, spend the rest of the afternoon in Lambertville and, if time permits, New Hope.

For those wishing to make a weekend of it all, there are two excellent bed & breakfasts in Lambertville—the Coryell House and the York Street House—plus a superb hotel, the Lambertville Inn, which possesses all the amenities of a first-class hotel, but with the cozy charm of a small inn.

In fact, this tour begins in the parking lot of the Lambertville Inn, located on the banks of the Delaware River off Bridge Street. Off to the side of the inn, the side opposite the river, is a gravel road that leads to the Delaware & Raritan Canal Towpath. The Towpath, as you'll recall if you've ridden the Stockton–Covered Bridge Tour or the Washington Crossing Tour, is a unique bicycle path.

The gravel road that leads to the Towpath often contains loose chunks of gravel and potholes. With the exception of Woodens Lane farther on in the tour, this gravel road is the worst road condition you'll encounter. If you own an all-terrain or mountain bike, you might consider using it for this tour. But a ten-speed with good tires will certainly do, too. You'll probably meet a few cyclists riding both kinds of bikes on the Towpath.

At the end of the gravel road, you'll come to a gate. It is there to prevent vehicles from riding on the Towpath. Walk your bike around the gate and resume riding. You will pass one mini-bridge over the Delaware & Raritan Canal on your left. The Delaware River is on your right. About a mile from the gate, you will find another bridge. Cross over this bridge and walk your bike up the short but steep path. You'll find yourself on the shoulder of Route 29.

Cross Route 29, but do so with caution because it is a busy road, especially in this section. You will now be at the base of Valley Road. Here you'll see an old stone barn and signs for Howell Farm and the Belle Mountain Ski area.

Valley Road is a long, winding hill that will take you to Howell Farm, your first stop. Along the way you'll pass the Belle Mountain Ski area on your right. At the intersection of Valley Road and Woodens Lane, approximately one and a half miles from the bottom of Valley Road, make a left, following signs to the entrance of Howell Farm.

Howell Farm is a "living history" farm. (See Longstreet Farm in the Holmdel Hustle tour.) A "living history" farm means that there are farm animals and fields of crops and that many of the chores are performed in a traditional, 19th-century manner. Run by the Mercer County Parks Commission, Howell Farm is also the site of occasional farm-related events such as a pumpkin-picking festival in October and hayrides.

Visit the farmhouse adjacent to the main barn and barnyard. These areas are typical of daily existence on a farm a century ago, and they reveal how a local farm family worked and lived.

Return to Woodens Lane, make a left, and go back to Valley Road. Make another left at Valley Road and continue down it to the "T" intersection with Pleasant Valley Road. Make yet another left and continue on Pleasant Valley Road.

The many rolling hills that you'll ride up and down throughout the next part of this tour possess some of the prettiest rural scenery in New Jersey. You'll pass many farms and fields, and don't be surprised if you spot a deer or two in the brush.

Your next turn, a left, will be onto Pleasant Valley-Harbourton Road, a couple of miles from the Valley Road/Pleasant Valley Road intersection. This is not a major intersection, so keep a sharp eye out for it. There is, however, a visible street sign.

Continue on Pleasant Valley-Harbourton Road. Cross over Route 579, the next intersection. Pleasant Valley–Harbourton Road now becomes Harbourton–Woodsville Road. You'll eventually come to another intersection where Harbourton–Woodsville Road intersects with Marshall's Corner Road. Make a left onto Marshall's Corner Road and proceed to the blinking traffic light and Route 518.

Route 518 is also known as the Lambertville-Hopewell Turnpike. Make a left onto Route 518. There will be a sign for Lambertville; it points in the direction you are headed.

Proceed on Route 518. It is a semi-busy road, so be careful. A few miles up on Route 518, you'll come to the Route 518 and Hunter Road–Rock Road intersection. (The left side of the intersection is Hunter Road; the right side is Rock Road.) You'll be able to identify the intersection because on your left is a bicycle shop called Wheel Fine Cycling. Make a right onto Rock Road. Rock Road will take you through a forested area of Hunterdon County. (Yes, you're back in Hunterdon County.) At the stop sign a few miles down the road, make a left. You'll now be on Mt. Airy-Harbourton Road, also known as Route 601.

Continue on Mt. Airy-Harbourton Road until the intersection with Rocktown-Lambertville Road. Make, what else, but a left. This road will take you straight into Lambertville, and it's all downhill.

At the stop sign on the edge of Lambertville, and the end of the Rocktown-Lambertville Road, make a right. This is a busy intersection; be wary of traffic. At the traffic light two hundred yards or so up ahead, make a left onto Bridge Street.

If there is too much traffic and not enough room to ride with safety, walk your bike through downtown Lambertville back to the Lambertville Station, a few short blocks away. On your right you'll pass the James Wilson Marshall House, the childhood home of the man who, with his partner Augustus Sutter, discovered gold in California in 1848. This discovery, of course, led to the famous California Gold Rush.

A block later you'll pass the Lambertville House, also on your right. Built in 1812, its guests included such great men in American history as President Andrew Johnson and General U. S. Grant.

Proceed on Bridge Street to the Lambertville Station and the Inn at the Lambertville Station where you'll make a left into the parking lot and conclude the tour.

13. Washington Crossing State Park

County: Mercer
Number of Miles: 8.5
Degree of Difficulty: Easy
Terrain: Mostly flat
Surface: Mostly good
Things to See: Delaware River, Delaware & Raritan Canal,
Nelson House, Titusville, Washington Crossing State Park,
Visitor's Center, Ferry House, George Washington Memorial
Arboretum

This tour is steeped in American history. At what is today Washington Crossing State Park, General George Washington and his Continental troops made their famous river-crossing on Christmas night 1776. Their attack on the Hessian mercenaries in Trenton was a turning point in America's battle for independence, according to most historians. Your tour is almost wholly within Washington Crossing State Park.

Located about midway between Lambertville and Trenton, Washington Crossing State Park is one of the state's prettiest parks. Beautifully maintained with much to see and do, the park is on the banks of the Delaware River and the land just beyond it and truly beckons bicyclists. Next to the park is the small, picturesque village of Titusville and a stretch of the Delaware & Raritan Canal and Towpath, all of which are included in this tour.

Since there is so much for the touring cyclist to experience here, if possible, plan to make a full day out of your bicycle ride and visit to the park. You'll certainly want to spend time at the Visitor's Center and other places of interest along the tour, and there are plenty of places to picnic.

If you come during the summer, you might want to stay for a play or concert at the Washington Crossing Open Air Theater located in the park. For information on theatrical and musical performances, call (609) 737-9721. Also, you might want to pedal over to Washington Crossing's sister park in Pennsylvania where

Nature Center

Nature Trails

To Nature Ctr.
(optional)

Knox
Grove
(optional)

Open Air Theater
(optional)

Titusville

Towpath

RTE. #29

Washington
Crossing
State Park

Park
Entrance

Canal

Visitor's
Ctr.

Delaware River

RIVER DR.

Ferry House
Tavern

Nursery

Memorial
Arboretum

RTE. #546

N

Nelson House

START
STOP

RTE. #29

Gate

How To Get There: Route 29 to the Route 546 intersection and the Washington Grove entrance to Washington Crossing State Park.

WASHINGTON CROSSING STATE PARK: DIRECTIONS AT A GLANCE

1. Washington Grove parking lot onto River Drive in Titusville.
2. River Drive to Delaware & Raritan Canal Towpath; return to Washington Grove via Towpath.
3. Cross Route 29. Route 546 to entrance; enter Washington Crossing State Park.
4. Left at second stop sign in park; proceed toward Visitor's Center. Enter Visitor's Center parking lot.
5. Right out of Visitor's Center parking lot and proceed to stop sign intersection. Follow signs for Nature Center, Knox Grove, and Open Air Theater. Follow road around this section of the park and back to the main entrance/exit road.
6. Cross main entrance/exit road, and once again, follow signs to Visitor's Center.
7. Do not turn into Visitor's Center parking lot. Instead continue to Ferry House Tavern and George Washington Memorial Arboretum. (Follow signs.)
8. Once again, return to main entrance/exit road. Make right at the stop sign and proceed out of the park.
9. Right onto Route 546.
10. Cross Route 29 and make a right into Washington Grove parking lot.

further history pertaining to Washington and his army and their daring winter crossing of the Delaware River awaits you.

The tour commences just outside the main section of Washington Crossing State Park, off Route 29 in what's known as Washington Grove. Directly opposite the road that leads to the formal entrance of the park (Route 546) is a bridge that spans the Delaware River and leads into Pennsylvania. If you're coming from Trenton, make a left at the traffic light, which is the Route 29–Route 546 intersection. Just before the bridge, which is not more than 200 yards away, is the entrance to Washington Grove. Make a right here. You will now be in the parking lot adjacent to the Nelson House.

(If you're coming from Lambertville and points north, make a right at the Route 29–Route 546 traffic light and then the quick right into Washington Grove as stated above. Do not go over the bridge.)

Before embarking on your ride, pay a brief visit to the Nelson House. The Nelson House was the landing point for the ferry to Pennsylvania before a covered bridge was built and made ferry service at this point on the river obsolete. The building served as the ferryman's residence as well as a tavern for those waiting on the ferry. Directly across from the Nelson House is the actual point where Washington and his troops landed on Christmas night 1776. The plaque located by this site explains to the visitor the details pertaining to the crossing.

Approximately 2,400 Continental soldiers crossed the river that night. With them, they brought supplies and eight cannon. After the battle in which 900 Hessians were captured and another 100 killed or wounded, Washington and his men, along with their Hessian captives, recrossed the Delaware at this point.

Once you've digested this bit of historical information, ride to the end of the parking lot, opposite its entrance. There you will find a scenic road, River Drive, which takes you along the Delaware and through the town of Titusville.

Titusville resembles a scene right out of a Norman Rockwell painting. Well-kept colonial homes hug the banks of the Delaware, and a sense of history and Americana surrounds the small community. It is only one and one half miles from the start of the tour to the north end of Titusville. At this point, you'll bear right and return back to the Nelson House and the Washington Grove parking lot. But this time you'll ride by way of the Delaware & Raritan Canal Towpath. The Towpath runs parallel to River Drive, but instead of being on the Delaware River, it is on the Delaware & Raritan Canal, located behind the river section of Titusville that you just rode through.

Do not go over the small canal bridge, located to the right of the conclusion of River Drive. If you do, you'll go onto Route 29, a busy highway too dangerous for cyclists, at least on this section of it. Just before the canal bridge, you'll see the Towpath. It will, most likely, have a wooden gate across it to prevent cars from entering. Simply walk your bicycle around it and ride the Towpath back to Washington Grove.

Upon completion of the Towpath section of the tour, make a left at the traffic light located at the Route 29–Route 546 intersection. Begin your pedal up the Route 546 hill to the formal entrance of Washington Crossing State Park, about three quarters of a mile away. Make a left into the entrance of the park. Pass the stop sign intersection a short distance away.

A few hundred feet farther is another intersection. Make a left here and follow signs to the Visitor's Center. Make another left into the Visitor's Center parking lot. Notice that the lot is located about 150 yards from the Visitor's Center building. Leave your locked bike in the parking lot and walk to the Visitor's Center, or walk with your bike along the path that leads to the building and lock it there.

In the Visitor's Center you'll be able to browse through two museum galleries that contain some 900 Revolutionary War artifacts. The North Gallery is comprised of items that deal with Washington's crossing of the Delaware and the Battle of Trenton. The theme of the South Gallery is New Jersey's role in the Revolution. The impressive collection of artifacts is chronological in arrangement. There are twelve sub-themes that begin with "Prelude to Revolution: 1758-73" and end with "Results of the Revolution: 1781-83."

There is also an electrical map that details the crossing and ensuing battle and a wonderful twenty-minute film that depicts in dramatic fashion still more crossing and battle information.

After you've spent some time in the Visitor's Center where you can also pick up free park maps and brochures, return to the parking lot area. Ride out of the parking lot, following the exit signs. Cross the intersection at the stop sign and continue to the Nature Center, Knox Grove, and Open Air Theater. At the bend in the road, you'll see the detour for the Nature Center. Visit it if you wish, but be advised that the road leading to it is not a good one.

Continue around the bend. Soon you'll come to the entrance to Knox Grove and the Open Air Theater. Once again, visit these if you wish. Knox Grove is a good place for a picnic in Washington Crossing State Park. It is situated on a loop road that will return you to where you are now.

Just beyond this point, on your right, you'll come to the Spring House. It's a small stone structure that once stood over a cold spring. Eighteenth-century farmers kept milk and other perishables in structures of this kind.

Proceed to the stop sign and the intersection of the park's main road. Cross the intersection; once again follow signs to the Visitor's Center. You have already cycled this stretch of the park. But rather than turning into the Visitor's Center parking lot as before, ride down the road to the Ferry House and Memorial Arboretum.

At the bottom of this road, you'll see the Ferry House Tavern. This is your next stop. It was here that General Washington set up his command post and discussed battle strategy with his officers on Christmas night. Across from the Ferry House is a stone barn from the original farm that was here during the Revolutionary War. Also near the Ferry House Tavern is the George Washington Memorial Arboretum; it contains trees and shrubs native to New Jersey.

Continue on this road, which passes the nursery north of the Arboretum. Pass, too, the Visitor's Center. Return to the next stop sign intersection. Make a right and ride to the park's exit. Make another right onto Route 546 and ride down the hill with caution. Cross the Route 29–Route 546 intersection at the light and return to the Nelson House and Washington Grove parking area where the tour began.

14. Cheesequake State Park

County: Monmouth
Number of Miles: 9.5
Degree of Difficulty: Easy
Terrain: Flat, except for Booth Field Road
Surface: Mostly good, except for Booth Field Road
Things to See: Cheesequake State Park natural areas, wildlife
    sanctuary, Hooks Lake

There are precious few scenic cycling areas in Middlesex County. Middlesex is a crossroads county; many of the state's major highways, including the Turnpike, Parkway, and Routes 287, 1, 9, and 18, intersect each other here. And recent development, both residential and commercial, has been widespread.

There is, however, a suitable cycling area in northeastern Middlesex County, despite all the activity around it. It's called Cheesequake State Park. The name "Cheesequake" can be traced back to the area's original inhabitants, the Leni-Lenape Indians. Although Cheesequake State Park is small in comparison to other state parks and possesses no historic sites or other attractions, it is, nonetheless, a good place to cycle, especially during the fall when the trees of Cheesequake explode with color.

Cheesequake is also easily accessible for bicyclists who live in Middlesex and upper Monmouth counties. It is an island in the middle of what is fast becoming New Jersey's newest urban area and, thus, can be enjoyed by a large number of bicycle tourists.

Actually, the Cheesequake State Park tour begins outside the park. If you arrive by car, park it in the commuter parking lot adjacent to the Exit 120 ramp off the Garden State Parkway South. You can also arrive at the lot via the Laurence Harbor Parkway, which crosses underneath the Garden State Parkway.

Exit the parking lot and bear right onto the Laurence Harbor Parkway, also known as Matawan Road. The road sign will say "Matawan and Old Bridge Township, Route 34." A quarter mile down the road, make a right at the traffic light onto Cliffwood Ave-

Arrowsmith Point
and Farry Point Picnic Area's
Parking

GARDEN

Restricted
Camping Area

Parking

STATE

PARKWAY

Hooks Creek
Lake

LAURENCE HARBOR
PKWY.

Park
Office
BOOTH
FIELD RD.
Park
Entrance

Parking

GORDON
RD.
START
STOP
CLIFFWOOD AVE.

N

How To Get There: Garden State Parkway, Exit 120
South, to Cheesequake Commuter Parking Lot.

CHEESEQUAKE: DIRECTIONS AT A GLANCE

1. Exit commuter parking lot. Right onto Laurence Harbor Parkway (Matawan Road).
2. Right at traffic light onto Cliffwood Avenue.
3. Right onto Gordon Road.
4. Bear right at first bend in road, after passing park headquarters.
5. Right at stop sign.
6. Bear left at next intersection. Head toward Arrowsmith Point and Farry Point.
7. U-turn in Farry Point parking area.
8. Proceed into Restricted Camping Area. Ride loop road.
9. Bear left at intersection just beyond Restricted Camping Area gates.
10. Left at stop sign.
11. Left onto Booth Field Road.
12. U-turn in Booth Field parking area.
13. Left onto main road in park.
14. Bear left at small island just beyond the entrance/exit road of park.
15. Proceed to Hooks Lake.
16. U-turn in Hooks Lake parking area.
17. Right at entrance/exit road intersection and proceed out of park onto Gordon Road.
18. Left onto Cliffwood Avenue.
19. Left onto Laurence Harbor Parkway (Matawan Road).

nue. Proceed a half mile or so to the stop sign. Make a right here onto Gordon Road. This road will lead to the entrance of the park.

Before proceeding into the park, stop at the Ranger Headquarters, which is located to the right of the park entrance booth. Pick up a Cheesequake park brochure and map. Exit the headquarters' parking lot and ride into Cheesequake.

Bear right at the first bend in the road and proceed to the "V"-shaped island in the middle of the road. There will also be a stop sign there. Make a right and continue farther into the park. You'll ride under both the southern and northern lanes of the Garden State Parkway.

At the next intersection, bear left and head toward Arrowsmith Point and Farry Point, two picnic areas in the northeast corner of Cheesequake. Pass through the Farry Point gates and pedal to the Farry Point picnic area, a half mile or so up the road.

Unlike most other parks that possess "loop" or circular roads and thus eliminate backtracking, Cheesequake has a series of roads that lead to a particular destination and dead end. Such is the case here. When you arrive at Farry Point, make a U-turn in the picnic area parking lot and return on the same road back to the intersection. Instead of bearing right, however, and following the signs to Hooks Lake and New Landing, continue straight and ride into the Restricted Camping Area. This is the only loop-like road in Cheesequake. It will take you on a quick tour of the campsites. Stay on the paved road and loop the campground. Once you're into the campground area, simply follow the exit signs and return to the same Restricted Camping Area gates you entered through.

Just beyond the gates is the intersection mentioned earlier. If you proceed straight, you'd head back to Farry Point. So, bear left and then make a left at the stop sign. Proceed under the Garden State Parkway again. Shortly thereafter is a road on your left that leads to the Booth Field Camping Area.

This road has had pothole problems in the past; there is no guarantee that your ride up this road will be a smooth and easy one. And you'll have to do a bit of climbing, since Booth Field sits atop a hill.

Those who prefer not to strain a bit or who decide against battling the possible potholes should bypass this road and continue toward Hooks Lake, your next destination. For those with a bit of adventure in their blood, make a left onto the Booth Field Road, pedal to the top, admire the foliage along the way as well as the tiny chipmunks that will scurry across the road in front of you, and then turn around and pedal on down.

Make a left back onto the main road and continue to Hooks Lake. You'll pass the road that leads back to the entrance/exit of the park. Bear left at the small island just beyond the entrance/exit road and follow signs to the lake.

There is swimming at Hooks Lake during the summer. There is also a large picnic area. If you plan to spend the day at Cheesequake, this is a good place for a respite. There are also several interesting hiking trails in the vicinity. Cheesequake is located in the "transition zone" of Northern and Southern New Jersey's vegetation regions. You'll find marsh areas, swamps, a sample of Pine Barrens forest, as well as a section of hardwood forest here.

As might be expected, on weekends this part of Cheesequake can get crowded, so plan accordingly. Turn around in the parking lot and backtrack to the entrance/exit road intersection. Make a right and proceed out of Cheesequake and onto Gordon Road. At the stop sign, make a left onto Cliffwood Avenue. At the traffic light, make another left onto Laurence Harbor Parkway (Matawan Road) and pedal back to the commuter parking lot where the tour began.

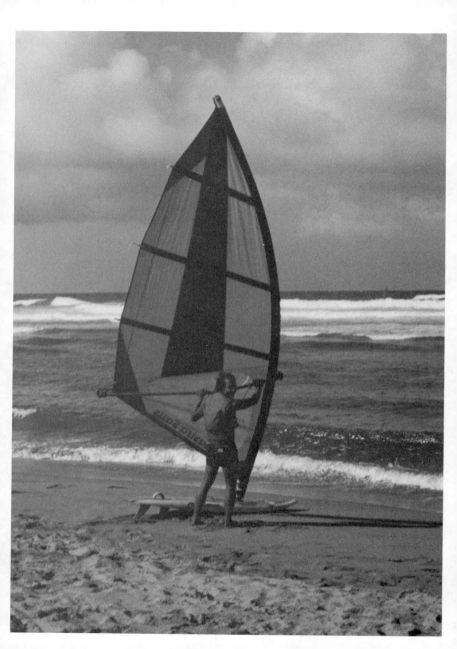

15. Highlands Hilltopper

County: Monmouth
Number of Miles: 6.2
Degree of Difficulty: Moderate to difficult
Terrain: Mostly hills, some steep
Surface: Good
Things to See: Atlantic Highlands, Scenic Drive, Mt. Mitchill,
    views of Sandy Hook and Sandy Hook Bay

Don't let the number of miles fool you. This is a short, but fairly strenuous tour. There are a number of tough hills on Ocean Boulevard. But for some bicyclists, the sweeping vistas at Mt. Mitchill and other points atop the Highlands make the effort worthwhile. The Highlands and the roads that comprise this tour are close to Sandy Hook and the Navesink River. (See tours of these two areas.) Cyclists interested in making a weekend out of touring might want to try all three tours or combine at least two of them into a good day's ride.

This tour concentrates on the scenic views of Sandy Hook and Sandy Hook Bay. It begins in the town of Atlantic Highlands, a popular boating and fishing outlet for charters, party boats, and private pleasure craft. The tour commences in the Municipal Harbor parking area at the very end of First Avenue. Park your car here.

Ride out of the parking area by way of Simon Lake Drive, which is the road closest to the docks. The Shore Casino, a noted Atlantic Highlands restaurant, will be on your left as you pass it. Proceed on Simon Lake Drive and ride around the bend where the view on a clear day is spectacular. Look for the Verrazano Bridge, Brooklyn, and Manhattan. At the conclusion of the bend Simon Lake Drive merges into First Avenue.

Ride down First Avenue to Ocean Boulevard a few hundred yards away. Make a left onto Ocean Boulevard, also known as Scenic Drive. Make your way up Ocean Boulevard. Be prepared for a long climb to the top.

Continue along Ocean Boulevard. Eventually you'll come to a fork in the road. Bear left. (If you go right, you'll be on East Highlands Road, which is a dead end.) Continue along Ocean Boulevard until you arrive at the Hofbrauhaus Restaurant.

SANDY HOOK BAY

How To Get There: Garden State Parkway, Exit 117, to Route 36 East. Follow signs to Sandy Hook. Just before Sandy Hook is Atlantic Highlands. Left on First Avenue in Atlantic Highlands to Municipal Harbor parking lot.

HIGHLANDS HILLTOPPER: DIRECTIONS AT A GLANCE

1. Parking area to Simon Lake Drive. Simon Lake Drive becomes First Avenue.
2. First Avenue to Ocean Boulevard. Left onto Ocean Boulevard.
3. Bear left at East Highlands Road fork.
4. Ocean Boulevard to Mt. Mitchill Scenic Overlook.
5. U-turn at Mt. Mitchill.
6. Left at Mt. Mitchill entrance/exit stop sign.
7. Right at next stop sign.
8. Cross Route 36 to Navesink Road.
9. Bear right onto Valley Drive. (Eventually Valley Drive becomes Memorial Parkway.)
10. Bear left at Route 36 intersection.
11. Right onto First Avenue.
12. First Avenue to Municipal Harbor parking area.

This is your first scenic stop. Although Mt. Mitchill is known for its wonderful views, the views of Sandy Hook and Sandy Hook Bay are actually better here than they are at Mt. Mitchill, your next stop. On a clear day, it is even possible to see the lower part of the New York skyline.

Continue along Ocean Boulevard until you reach the entrance to Mt. Mitchill Scenic Overlook, part of the Monmouth County Parks System. Mt. Mitchill is the highest point on the Eastern Seaboard; it rises 266 feet above sea level. Once again you'll enjoy a grand sight of Sandy Hook and its bay, provided that the park's attendants have cleared the brush and tree limbs that frequently hamper the view.

Turn around and return to Mt. Mitchill Scenic Overlook entrance/exit. There is a stop sign here. Make a left. Ride down the small hill to the next stop sign. This time make a right and ride to the Route 36 traffic light. Signs will point to Red Bank. Cross Route 36. You'll now be on Navesink Avenue, also called Route 8B. On your left you'll pass Hartshorne Woods Park.

Continue on Navesink Avenue to the intersection where Locust Avenue, Monmouth Avenue, and Valley Drive (also called Route 8A) meet. Bear right and proceed on Valley Drive. Eventually Valley Drive turns into Memorial Parkway.

A mile or so up the road is the Route 36 intersection. Here Route 36 and Memorial Parkway become one. Bear left onto Route 36 (Memorial Parkway), but do so with caution. This is a major thoroughfare. However, it is the only way to get back to the downtown area of Atlantic Highlands and the Municipal Harbor parking area where the tour began.

Proceed on Route 36 West to the traffic light at the First Avenue intersection. Make a right onto First Avenue and ride to the end of it where the Municipal parking area is located. This is the end of the tour.

16. Navesink River Ramble

County: Monmouth
Number of Miles: 11.7
Degree of Difficulty: Moderate
Terrain: Some hills
Surface: Mostly good
Things to See: Navesink River, Locust, British Retreat Route of
    1778

The town of Rumson and the Navesink River area of Middletown
are two of the prettiest, and wealthiest, parts of the North Jersey
Shore; million-dollar mansions are not uncommon. The close prox-
imity to New York and the industrial centers of North Jersey as well
as the Shore's beach and boating areas make this an ideal place to
live—if you can afford it.

Happily, it costs nothing to ride through this picturesque area
on your bicycle. The tour commences at the intersection of
Bingham and River roads in Rumson. Bingham Road is also
known as Route 8A. Head north on Route 8A toward the river. Just
prior to the Oceanic Bridge, which spans the Navesink River, you'll
pass the Fisherman's Wharf Restaurant on your left. Ride over the
Oceanic Bridge. To your right is the Navesink's outlet to Sandy
Hook Bay.

Once you're off the bridge, you'll round the bend that hugs
the Navesink River and make a right at the intersection. This is still
Route 8A, but now you're in Locust, not Rumson. Locust is a historic district of Middletown. It was settled in the late eighteenth
century. Originally, it was an oyster and shellfish village, but over
the years it became a summer resort for New York artists and theatrical performers.

Make a right onto Locust Avenue, which is a continuation of
Route 8A. Cross over the small bridge, and at the intersection of
Route 8A and 8B, make a left onto Monmouth Avenue, which later
turns into King's Highway East. It was here that British forces, flee-
ing the Continental Army of General George Washington after the
Battle of Monmouth in June 1778 (see Monmouth Battlefield tour),

How To Get There: Garden State Parkway, Exit 109, to Newman Springs Road. Left on Broad Street. Right on Front Street/River Road to River Road-Bingham intersection in Rumson.

NAVESINK RIVER RAMBLE: DIRECTIONS AT A GLANCE

1. Route 8A, over Oceanic Bridge.
2. Right at intersection (still Route 8A).
3. Right onto Locust Avenue.
4. Left onto Monmouth Avenue/King's Highway East.
5. Left onto Sleepy Hollow Road.
6. Right onto Chapel Hill Road.
7. Left back onto Sleepy Hollow Road.
8. Left onto Cooper Road.
9. Right onto Patterson Lane.
10. Left onto Navesink River Road (Route 12A).
11. Right onto Route 8A, back over Oceanic Bridge.

camped while awaiting boats to arrive at nearby Sandy Hook. From Sandy Hook the British escaped to New York, thanks to the help of local Tories. This road was also a common trail (the Minnisink Trail) used by local Indians.

Proceed on Monmouth Avenue/King's Highway East. You'll notice that the old properties found in Locust gradually give way to new homes and developments located in the Chapel Hill section of Middletown. In earlier times most of the land on which the newer homes now stand were grazing pastures and part of the many horse farms that dotted Middletown.

At the King's Highway–Sleepy Hollow Road traffic light intersection, make a left onto Sleepy Hollow Road. You'll notice on your right signs that state: "U.S. Government Property. No Trespassing." Behind the fence is a skinny stretch of property on which is located a military-only railroad. The railroad connects two sections of the U.S. Naval Weapons Station at Earle.

At the "T" intersection and stop sign, make a right onto Chapel Hill Road and then a fast left back onto another section of Sleepy Hollow Road. You'll come to another "T" intersection and another stop sign. Make a left here onto Cooper Road. Three streets later, make a right onto Patterson Lane.

Patterson Lane isn't paved, but it is usually kept in good condition. It's only a short distance that you'll have to ride on Patterson Lane, anyway. At the end of it, you'll come to yet another "T" intersection and stop sign. Make a left onto Navesink River Road, also called Route 12A.

Navesink River Road is certainly the most scenic road on this tour. Be prepared for some hills, though. To your right is the Navesink River, and all around you are million-dollar properties. You'll pass the Navesink Country Club and its golf course on your left and delightful views of the river on your right.

Continue on Navesink River Road (Route 12A) to the blinking light about three miles or so down the road. At the blinking light make a right back onto Route 8A. Round the bend and go back over the Oceanic Bridge to your starting point in Rumson at the corner of Route 8A (Bingham Road) and River Road. The tour concludes here.

17. Holmdel Hustle

County: Monmouth
Number of Miles: 12.9
Degree of Difficulty: Moderate to difficult
Terrain: Hilly
Surface: Good
Things to See: Tatum Park, Holmes-Hendrickson House, Holmdel
Park, Longstreet Farm

Holmdel is a large, semi-rural community located in upper Monmouth County. Home of the Garden State Arts Center, Bell Labs, sprawling parks, million-dollar homes, and long, winding country roads, Holmdel can be a bicyclist's delight. The Garden State Parkway cuts right through the center of Holmdel; thus, the township and the tour of it described below are easily accessible for those arriving by car.

Although the roads on this tour are in a semi-rural setting, they are not free of traffic. Holmdel is a growing community, and development is in full stride. Therefore, be certain to abide by the rules of the road and ride with caution. Some roads on this tour do not have standard shoulders, so stay as far to the right as possible, especially when negotiating bends and turns where you might not be visible to approaching vehicles.

The tour begins in the parking lot of the Special Services Section of Tatum Park, located off Holland Road. Proceed out of the parking lot and turn left onto Holland Road. Pass through the traffic light at the intersection of Holland Road and Laurel Avenue, and continue on Holland to South Holland Road about a mile away.

Make a left onto South Holland Road. To your right will be the grounds of the Garden State Arts Center. Cross underneath the Garden State Parkway.

There is a "T" intersection at the end of South Holland Road. Make a right onto Crawford's Corner/Everett Road. Proceed a short distance, perhaps 300 yards or so, to the Longstreet Road traffic light. Make a left onto Longstreet Road. A quarter mile from the traffic light, you'll pass the Holmdel Activity Center on your right.

How To Get There: Garden State Parkway, Exit 114. Red Hill Road to Van Schoick Road. Right on Holland Road to entrance of Special Services Section of Tatum Park.

HOLMDEL HUSTLE: DIRECTIONS AT A GLANCE

1. Left onto Holland Road.
2. Left onto South Holland Road.
3. Right onto Crawford's Corner/Everett Road.
4. Left onto Longstreet Road.
5. Left onto Robert's Road.
6. Right onto Crawford's Corner/Everett Road.
7. Right onto Middletown Road.
8. Left onto Stilwell Road.
9. Left onto Middletown–Lincroft Road.
10. Left onto Holland Road.
11. Left into entrance of Special Services Section of Tatum Park.

Farther down the road, also on your right and just prior to Holmdel Park, is the Holmes-Hendrickson House, your first stop.

This restored Dutch-English house, built in 1754, is open to the public, but on a limited basis. Guides are there June through October, but only four days a week. (Call 908–462–1466 for details.)

In the Holmes-Hendrickson House are colonial kitchen displays, antique furniture, and farm tools. The guide will explain to you the history of the house and its importance in depicting the integration of Dutch and English customs by colonists.

Immediately after the Holmes-Hendrickson House is the entrance to Holmdel Park and Longstreet Farm. Be certain to allow some time here. Longstreet Farm is a working, "living history" farm, one that was prosperous from the mid-1700s to the 1920s and was owned by one of the first Dutch families to settle in Monmouth County. Today, Longstreet Farm is maintained by the Monmouth County Parks Commission.

In the various barns and farm buildings you'll view turn-of-the-century farm machines and Victorian carriages. Park employees dressed in Victorian garb perform routine farm chores the same way they were performed one hundred years ago.

Do be sure to tour the Longstreet Farm farmhouse, which has been restored and is decorated in delightful Victorian style. The last of the Longstreets were gentlemen farmers, and their wealth is evident here.

After your visit to Holmdel Park's Longstreet Farm, ride out the park's exit and back onto Longstreet Road. Ride to the intersection of Longstreet Road and Robert's Road. Make a left onto Robert's Road and ride to the Crawford's Corner/Everett Road intersection. Make a right onto Crawford's Corner/Everett Road.

Proceed on Crawford's Corner/Everett Road. On your right is the huge Bell Labs complex. Near the Bell Labs tower you'll find a plaque that commemorates the discovery of radio waves from outer space by Bell Labs scientist Karl Jansky in 1982. The discovery began the science of radio astronomy.

At the traffic light, make a right onto Middletown Road. (The road to the left of the light, opposite Middletown Road, is called Red Hill Road.) Proceed to the bend in the road where you'll find an intersection. Make a left here. This road is called Stilwell Road, although it is not marked as such at this intersection.

Proceed to the Crawford's Corner/Everett Road intersection. (You have completed a loop; that's why you're back at Crawford's Corner/Everett Road.) Cross Crawford's Corner/Everett Road. Stilwell Road now becomes Sunnyside Road. On both sides of the road is the Bamm Hollow Country Club.

At the Middletown–Lincroft Road intersection there is a stop sign. Make a left here onto Middletown–Lincroft Road. Once again, you'll pass under the Garden State Parkway, a short distance up the road. Proceed through the traffic light at Dwight Road/Nut Swamp Road and Middletown–Lincroft Road. This is the route British soldiers under General Sir Henry Clinton used to make their retreat from Washington's Continental forces after the Battle of Monmouth in June 1778. (See Monmouth Battlefield tour.) The British ultimately made it to Sandy Hook and boarded boats and crossed lower New York Harbor to Manhattan and safety.

Pass through the Bamm Hollow/Oak Hill Road and Middletown–Lincroft Road intersection where another traffic light is located. Continue on Middletown–Lincroft Road. Pass the Middletown Railroad Station on your right. Immediately after the station, make a left onto Holland Road. If you come to the railroad tracks that cut across Middletown-Lincroft Road, you missed the left turn onto Holland Road.

Pass through the stop sign intersection at Holland and Red Hill Road. Continue on Holland to the entrance of the Special Services Section of Tatum Park, the tour's starting point. Make a left into Tatum Park and proceed to the parking lot.

18. Monmouth Battlefield

County: Monmouth
Number of Miles: 8.7
Degree of Difficulty: Easy
Terrain: Flat
Surface: Good
Things to See: Monmouth Battlefield State Park, Visitor's Center,
    Battlefield Orchards, Molly Pitcher's Well, Owl Haven Nature
    Center, Old Tennent Church

The Battle of Monmouth was a crucial Revolutionary War engagement fought between General George Washington's Continental Army and British regulars. It occurred on June 28, 1778. Washington's victory at Monmouth enabled him to rally the American forces and fellow patriots after a brutal, demoralizing winter spent at Valley Forge.

Much of the battlefield is now part of Monmouth Battlefield State Park. Located in Freehold on Route 33, just off the Freehold Circle, the park is well worth a visit. To explore it and its surrounding points of interest by bicycle is the most rewarding way to step back into history.

Before you do any cycling, be certain first to spend some time in the Monmouth Battlefield State Park Visitor's Center. Since Monmouth Battlefield is one of New Jersey's newest state parks, the facilities are modern and the displays are wonderfully presented and most informative. There are self-operated slide presentations and a large electronic map that tells the story of the strategies and troop movements during this pivotal battle. There is also a small gift stand where visitors can purchase souvenirs and additional material on the battle as well as pick up free park maps and brochures.

There are some twenty-five miles worth of walking tours and bicycle paths in the park. Cyclists can spend a good part of a morning leisurely riding the park trail network, so do bring lunch if you plan to spend the day. Use one of the free park maps available at the Visitor's Center to plan your ride within the park.

TENNENT RD.

☐ Old Tennent Church

COUNTY RD. #3
(Main St.)

RTE. #522

Owl Haven
☐ Nature Center

☐
Molly Pitcher's
Well

MILLHURST RD.

START
STOP

☐ Visitors
Center

WEMROCK RD.

☐ Battleview
Orchards

→ RTE. #33

N

How To Get There: Route 9 to the Freehold Circle. Route 33 West to the entrance to Monmouth Battlefield State Park.

MONMOUTH BATTLEFIELD: DIRECTIONS AT A GLANCE

1. Out Monmouth Battlefield State Park and left onto Route 33.
2. Left onto Wemrock Road.
3. Left onto Route 522.
4. Right onto Tennent Road. Visit Old Tennent Church.
5. Return to Tennent Road. Cross Route 522. Tennent Road becomes Main Street. (County Road #3). Proceed on Main Street.
6. Left onto Millhurst Road.
7. Left onto Route 33.
8. Left back into Monmouth Battlefield State Park. Ride to Visitor's Center parking lot.

The Monmouth Battlefield tour described below deals mostly with the roads and things to see just outside the park. Perhaps the best way to enjoy the Monmouth Battlefield experience on bike is to arrive early in the morning, spend some time at the Visitor's Center, ride the park's paths, have a picnic lunch, and then ride the tour described below.

Park your car in the Visitor's Center parking lot. Follow the exit signs out of the park. At the park's entrance/exit, make a left onto Route 33. Be advised that this is a heavy-use road, so proceed with caution. Make a left at the traffic light onto Wemrock Road.

A short distance from this intersection is Battleview Orchards, a popular apple, peach, and pumpkin "pick-your-own" farm. You can also purchase some of New Jersey's finest apple cider here in the fall as well as apple pies, apple cider donuts, and Battleview jam and jelly.

Proceed on Wemrock Road after your stop at Battleview Orchards. You'll pass Battleview's apple orchards and the remains of an old farm. At the stop sign, which is the intersection of Wemrock Road and Route 522, make a left. Once again, ride with caution, since this is a frequently traveled road.

Approximately a quarter mile from the Wemrock Road–Route 522 intersection on the left side of the road is the famous Molly Pitcher's Well. It was Molly Pitcher, according to legend, who gave water to thirsty patriots during the Battle of Monmouth. And when her husband was wounded, Molly took his place beside his cannon. Because of her valor, it is said Molly Pitcher was made an honorary officer in the Continental Army.

The well on Route 522, although called Molly Pitcher's Well and celebrated as such, is not, say historians, the actual well where Molly Pitcher drew water during the Battle of Monmouth. That well, as the plaque on Route 522 will tell you, is located some 200 yards to the east.

Your next stop on Route 522 is the Owl Haven Nature Center. It is located about half a mile from Molly Pitcher's Well on the right side of the road. Run by the New Jersey Audubon Society, Owl Haven contains numerous environmental exhibits. It's worth a stop.

Leave the Owl Haven Nature Center parking lot and continue west on Route 522. At the traffic light, which is the intersection of Route 522 and Tennent Road, make a right and ride to the Old Tennent Church. It's located a few hundred yards from the intersection on your right. It was here that a hospital was set up to care for the American wounded during the Battle of Monmouth. In the cemetery that surrounds the front and sides of the church are the remains of American and British soldiers killed in the battle.

Go back to the traffic light at the Route 522 and Tennent Road intersection. Just beyond the light, Tennent Road becomes Main Street, or County Road #3. Proceed down this road to the Millhurst Road (Route 527) intersection. Make a left onto Millhurst Road. Proceed south to the Route 33 intersection.

Make sure you keep to your right just after you turn left at the intersection. It will seem as if you are pedaling onto a major highway, given the nature of the entrance onto Route 33. Proceed with caution, since there are no shoulders on the entrance ramp. However, once you're off the ramp (it's no more than a hundred yards or so) and actually on the main section of Route 33, you will be able to cycle within a wide shoulder area back to the Monmouth Battlefield State Park entrance.

Once inside the park, proceed to the Visitor's Center parking lot where the tour concludes.

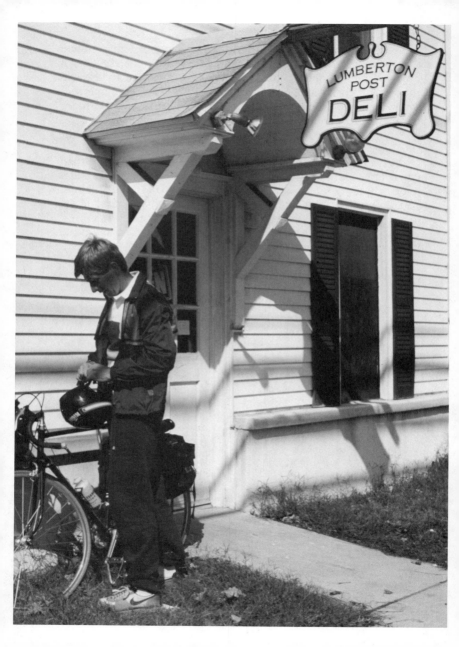

19. Allaire

County: Monmouth
Number of Miles: 8.8
Degree of Difficulty: Easy
Terrain: Flat
Surface: Mostly good
Things to See: Allaire State Park, Deserted Village, Pine Creek
Railroad

Allaire State Park is yet another one of those state parks that you
will want to spend some time in, either before or after you complete this bicycle tour. There is much to see and do here. Although
the tour begins and ends in the park, virtually all of the tour is on
roads outside it. Even though Allaire offers much to the park visitor,
bicycling, unfortunately, isn't one of them. There are few paths or
designated bike routes in the park.

But just outside the park is a good network of roads that
winds through parts of lower Monmouth County. In order to make
Allaire the starting and stopping points on the tour, I selected those
roads that form a loop around the park. I suggest that you arrive
at Allaire early, complete your bike tour, and then spend the remainder of the day strolling about Allaire's Deserted Village and
enjoying the park's other attractions. Any season except winter is a
good one to visit Allaire.

Back in the early 1800s Allaire was a profitable iron ore community. Its big furnaces and the craftsmen who lived and worked in
the village turned out such useful household iron products as cal-
drons, pots, kettles, stoves, and piping. More than 450 people lived
and worked at Allaire during the community's peak years, which
occurred in the 1820s and 1830s.

Actually, Allaire thrived until 1846. It was in this year, though,
that coal was discovered in Pennsylvania's Allegheny Mountains.
Bog iron foundries such as Allaire and Batsto, located farther south
in the heart of the Pine Barrens (See the Pine Barrens tour), burned
charcoal from pitch pine in their huge furnaces. But it was quickly
learned that coal was cheaper to use than charcoal. As a result, in

How To Get There: Garden State Parkway, Exit 98, to Route 34 South, to Allenwood Road, to Route 524 West. Left into Allaire State Park.

ALLAIRE: DIRECTIONS AT A GLANCE

1. Leaving Allaire State Park, left onto Route 524 (Atlantic Avenue).
2. Left onto Route 547 (Lakewood–Farmingdale Road).
3. Left onto Easy Street. (Easy Street becomes Hospital Road.)
4. Left onto Route 524 (Atlantic Avenue).
5. Left back into Allaire State Park.

only a few years, Allaire Village became known as the Deserted Village.

Fortunately, much of the village has been restored. And today you can wander back into history and gain a good understanding of what living and working in a nineteenth-century bog-iron community was like. In the village, you can, for instance, visit the blacksmith shop, general store, and chapel where visitors may still attend services on Sunday.

Adjacent to the village is the Pine Creek Railroad and the Pine Creek Rail Museum. Take a ride on the railroad and its antique railcars, or go for an old-fashioned wagon ride, which departs regularly just outside the Allaire Visitor's Center.

During the spring, summer, and fall, weekends at Allaire are almost always made up of a special event or two. Flea markets, antique shows, craft fairs, and art exhibits are common. Camping, canoeing, horseback riding, and picnicking are also popular at Allaire. Call (908) 938–2371 for a schedule of events.

To start the bicycle tour, park your car in the parking lot opposite the Pine Creek Railroad and in front of the Allaire Visitor's Center. Pedal out the park's exit to Route 524. Make a left onto Route 524, which is also known as Atlantic Avenue. A mile up Route 524, you'll pass the entrance to the Allaire State Park campgrounds.

At the traffic light, which is at the Route 524–Route 547 intersection, make a left. This is a fairly busy intersection because just down the road on Route 547 is an entrance to a major highway, Route 195. Proceed with caution. Bear to your left and follow signs for Route 547 South. Pass through the Herbertsville Road traffic light. The next left you can make will be on Easy Street. Turn here. On Easy Street you'll pass small horse and chicken farms. Years ago this entire area consisted of nothing but farms. But Monmouth County has experienced a tremendous growth spurt in the last twenty years, and farmland is rapidly disappearing.

You'll pass through three stop signs before Easy Street becomes Hospital Road. The first stop sign is at the Newton's Corner intersection. The second is at the Herbertsville Road intersection. And the third is at the Squankum Road intersection. All of these occur in rather quick succession; it's barely a half mile from the first to the last stop sign.

Proceed on what is now Hospital Road. Allaire State Park property is on both sides of the road. At the next stop sign, which is located at the Hospital Road–Route 524 (Atlantic Avenue) intersection, make a left. You'll pass the Spring Meadow Golf Course, the only state-owned golf course in New Jersey. Continue on Route 524 (Atlantic Avenue) to the entrance of Allaire State Park. Ride with caution: Route 524 is a busy road on weekends.

Make a left at the entrance to Allaire State Park and ride back to the main parking lot. The tour concludes here.

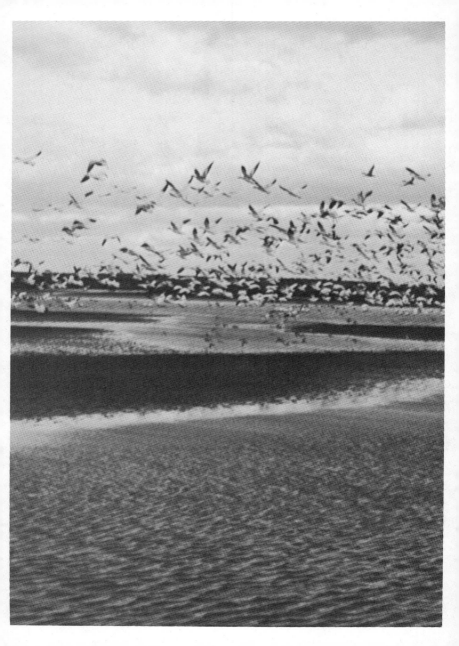

20. Sandy Hook

County: Monmouth
Number of Miles: 10.3
Degree of Difficulty: Easy
Terrain: Flat
Surface: Good
Things to See: Spermaceti Visitor's Center, Old Dune Trail,
    Battery Gunnison, Sandy Hook Lighthouse, Fort Hancock,
    Sandy Hook Museum, History House, Halyburton
    Monument, salt marsh, Sandy Hook Bay

Sandy Hook is the New Jersey unit of Gateway National Recreation
Area. A skinny, shifting, sandspit peninsula on the uppermost reach
of the Jersey Shore, Sandy Hook offers a variety of attractions and
pleasant cycling. Plan to spend a full day here.

Those who cycle onto Sandy Hook will be allowed into the
park free. However, those who drive a vehicle in will be charged an
admission fee. If you drive, arrive early during the summer months
and on weekends. Sandy Hook fills up quickly, and once the parking lots are full, the park is closed to vehicles.

Park your car in Parking Area "B," located just beyond the entrance to Sandy Hook. Start your tour of Sandy Hook by exiting the
parking area and making a right onto Hartshorne Drive, Sandy
Hook's main thoroughfare. On your right, just beyond the seawall,
is the Atlantic Ocean. To your left is Sandy Hook Bay.

It is approximately two miles to the Spermaceti Visitor's Center.
Stop here to view the free slide show that details the natural
history and military importance of Sandy Hook. There are also exhibits that pertain to the wildlife found on the Hook and displays
of old lifesaving apparatus. Finally, don't leave without picking up
the free brochures available at the Ranger's desk. These brochures
will enlighten you on Sandy Hook's delicate ecological makeup.
Such information will make your bike tour that much more
rewarding.

Just beyond the parking area of the Spermaceti Visitor's Center
is the Old Dune Trail, a one-mile loop that provides a good intro-

How To Get There: Exit 117 off the Garden State Parkway. Route 36 East to Gateway National Recreation Area (Sandy Hook).

SANDY HOOK: DIRECTIONS AT A GLANCE

1. Right out of Parking Area "B" onto Hartshorne Drive.
2. Visit Spermaceti Visitor's Center.
3. Right onto Atlantic Drive.
4. Follow road onto Gunnison Road.
5. Right onto Magruder Road.
6. Bear right at the fork 50 yards later onto Hudson Drive.
7. Visit Sandy Hook Lighthouse.
8. Return to Magruder Road. Right onto Magruder.
9. Left at stop sign, some 200 feet later. Follow "Museum" signs.
10. Visit Sandy Hook Museum. (Located on Kearney Road.)
11. Continue on Kearney Road. Left at yield sign onto Hartshorne Drive.
12. Hartshorne Drive to Parking Area "B."

duction to the Sandy Hook landscape. Stay on the trail. Poison ivy abounds. Also, keep an eye out for the many birds that use Sandy Hook as a respite, since the peninsula sits on the Atlantic Flyway. In addition to sighting common shore birds, you might also catch a glimpse of an osprey, a yellow-bellied sapsucker, or a red-headed woodpecker.

Exit the parking area of the Spermaceti Visitor's Center and make a right onto Hartshorne Drive. Continue to the Hartshorne Drive/Atlantic Drive intersection. Make a right onto Atlantic Drive and head toward Gunnison and North Beaches. Along the way you'll see various shrubs, trees, and barrier beach plants indigenous to Sandy Hook.

Atlantic Drive eventually veers to the right. Stay on Gunnison Road. Located on Gunnison Road is Battery Gunnison, a good example of the defense emplacements found on Sandy Hook earlier in the century. You'll see here the remains of two six-inch gun batteries built in 1904.

Proceed on Gunnison Road to Magruder Road. Make a right onto Magruder Road. You will now be entering the Fort Hancock area of Sandy Hook. Approximately fifty yards later, bear right at the fork in the road onto Hudson Drive. To your left you'll see the Sandy Hook Lighthouse. Built in 1764, the Sandy Hook Light is America's oldest operating lighthouse. Visitors are not permitted to enter the lighthouse, however.

Turn around and go back to the Magruder Road stop sign. Make a right onto Magruder. Approximately two hundred feet later is another stop sign. Make a left at this intersection. On your right will be the Brookdale Community College Environmental Study Center. On your left will be the Pershing Parade Field. Bear to your right and follow "Museum" signs.

The next point of interest is the Sandy Hook Museum. It is located to your right and contains exhibits, maps, and memorabilia of Fort Hancock. The fort was an important part of America's coastal defense during World Wars One and Two. It protected the entrance to New York Harbor.

After visiting the museum, make a right on Kearney Road (the road that the museum is located on). At the yield sign where the Rodman Gun is located, make a left back onto Hartshorne Drive.

The Rodman Gun, a huge Civil War-era cannon, is a Sandy Hook landmark. It is only one of two that still exist today.

Make a brief stop at the History House (Building #1) on that section of Hartshorne Drive known as "Officer's Row." The one-time residence of a lieutenant and his family stationed at Fort Hancock at the turn of the century, the History House is furnished with period pieces and is worth a visit.

Proceed south on Hartshorne Drive. Bear right where the Nike missiles are located at the fort's exit. These weapons serve as a reminder of Sandy Hook's importance as a strategic air defense post in the 1950s.

Continue south on Hartshorne Drive. On your left you'll pass the Halyburton Monument, where excavators found the remains of British sailors from the Revolutionary War. Continue south on Hartshorne Drive. The salt marshes of Sandy Hook Bay and a good view of the Highlands will be on your right. The fort-like structure found at the very top of the Highlands is the Twin Lights Historical Site, one of America's most unusual lighthouses and the home of an excellent museum.

Continue south on Hartshorne Drive until you return to Parking Area "B."

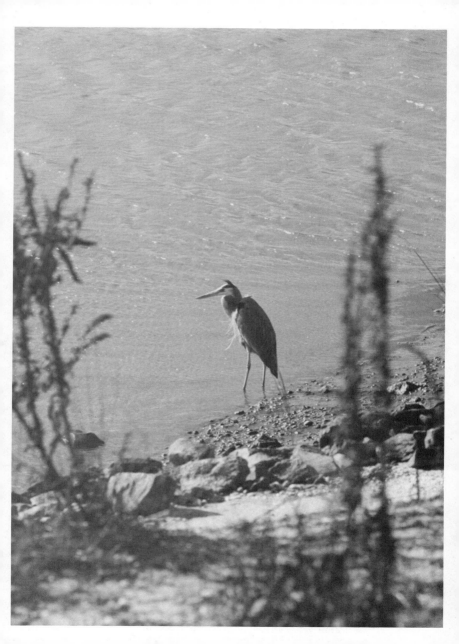

21. The Barnegat Peninsula

County: Ocean
Number of Miles: 25
Degree of Difficulty: Easy
Terrain: Flat
Surface: Good
Things to See: Manasquan Inlet, Point Pleasant Beach fishing
    fleet, Jersey Shore resort towns of Bay Head and
    Mantoloking, Barnegat Bay

The Barnegat Peninsula extends from Point Pleasant Beach down
to the tip of Island Beach State Park and is virtually surrounded by
water. The peninsula sits between two inlets—the Manasquan and
the Barnegat—and is flanked by the Atlantic Ocean to the east and
Barnegat Bay to the west. The peninsula's only connection to main-
land New Jersey is where Point Pleasant Beach meets Point Pleasant Boro, just north of Barnegat Bay.

    This tour is an early-morning-summer or weekends-in-Septem-
ber tour. The resort towns that line the peninsula, from Point Pleasant Beach to Seaside Park, are alive with activity and vacationers
from June through August. Needless to say, vehicle and pedestrian
traffic gets heavy during the day as families make their way to the
beaches and boardwalks that the Barnegat Peninsula is noted for.

    You can enjoy a bicycle tour of the peninsula—if you ride early
in the morning. Not only is traffic light then, but the wind is still and
the sun does not reach its most potent position in the sky until
noon.

    The tour commences in the parking lot that runs along the
Point Pleasant Beach section of the Manasquan Inlet. To park here,
you must arrive early. The inlet is a popular fishing spot, and an-
glers are usually early risers. If there are no spaces left, you can
park in Jenkinson's parking lot, which is adjacent to the inlet parking lot. There is a fee to park in Jenkinson's.

    Make a right out of whichever lot you find a space in and ride
around the U-shaped Inlet Drive. You'll pass the Manasquan Inlet
Coast Guard Station and Point Pleasant Beach's commercial fishing

How To Get There: Garden State Parkway, Exit 98, to Route 34 South. Route 34 South to Route 35 South to Broadway in Point Pleasant Beach. Broadway to Inlet Drive.

BARNEGAT PENINSULA: DIRECTIONS AT A GLANCE

1. Right out of Manasquan Inlet parking lot onto Inlet Drive.
2. Left at the stop sign and immediately bear right as you enter onto Ocean Avenue.
3. Proceed down Ocean Avenue through Point Pleasant Beach to Bay Head boundary traffic light (where Ocean Avenue meets Route 35). Make left.
4. Left at next traffic light (Osborne Avenue) onto East Avenue.
5. East Avenue to its conclusion at Lyman Street.
6. Right on Lyman, then left onto Route 35 South.
7. Route 35 South, pass the start of the divided highway (Route 35 into separate north and south lanes).
8. Right onto Ortley Avenue in Lavallette, then bear left onto Bay Boulevard.
9. Bay Boulevard to Harding Avenue. Make left onto Harding.
10. Cross Route 35 South. Left onto Route 35 North, also called Grand Central Avenue.
11. North onto Route 35 through Lavallette, Ocean Beach, Normandy Beach and into Mantoloking.
12. Left at Mantoloking Bridge traffic light.
13. Right onto Barnegat Lane. (Becomes Clayton Avenue in Bay Head.)
14. Bear right onto Johnson Avenue at conclusion of Barnegat Lane. Make left onto Lake Avenue in Bay Head.
15. Lake Avenue to Osborne Avenue. Make a right, then a left onto Route 35 North.
16 Bear right at next traffic light and onto Ocean Avenue.
17. Ocean Avenue to Inlet Drive and Manasquan Inlet parking lot.

fleet. At the stop sign, make a left and immediately bear right onto Ocean Avenue. There are no shoulders on Ocean Avenue but plenty of parked cars in the summer. Ride with caution. Once you pass the Arnold Avenue traffic light about a mile away, Ocean Avenue becomes less congested. At that point you'll also get a glimpse of Point Pleasant Beach's boardwalk and amusement rides.

Continue on Ocean Avenue until the end of Point Pleasant Beach and the beginning of Bay Head, one of the Shore's prettiest resort towns. At the "T" intersection traffic light where Ocean Avenue meets Route 35, make a left. Follow signs for Bay Head, Mantoloking, and Seaside Heights. At the next traffic light, some two hundred yards away, make a left onto Osborne Avenue which quickly leads you onto East Avenue.

Proceed down East Avenue through the towns of Bay Head and Mantoloking. You will see million-dollar mansions on the beach side of East Avenue. Once again, ride with caution. Beachgoers must cross East Avenue to get to the sand and surf.

East Avenue eventually runs into Lyman Street. Make a right onto Lyman, go one block to the Route 35 intersection, and make a left. Route 35 is the Barnegat Peninsula's main artery. Although it's a busy road, Route 35 does have shoulders suitable for cycling. Nonetheless, ride with caution.

Proceed on Route 35 South through Mantoloking and then into the southern section of the Barnegat Peninsula. You'll know you're there because Route 35 goes from two to four lanes. The two southbound lanes run parallel to Barnegat Bay, while the two north-bound lanes are closer to the beach. At that point where Route 35 divides into separate north- and south-bound lanes, simply bear right and remain on Route 35 South. The shoulder will become even wider, and you'll have a great view of the bay as you pass through the small summer resort towns of Normandy and Ocean Beaches, Lavallette, and finally Ortley Beach.

Stay on Route 35 South until you enter the town of Lavallette, approximately five miles from the point where Route 35 divided into separate north and south lanes. Make a right onto Ortley Avenue, go one block, and turn left onto Bay Boulevard. Bay Boulevard hugs Barnegat Bay and continues into the town of Ortley Beach.

Just prior to the Ortley Beach-Seaside Heights border is Harding Avenue. Make a left onto Harding. Cross over Route 35 South.

A block or two later is the Route 35 North intersection. Make a left here. In Ortley, Route 35 North is also called Grand Central Avenue.

You are now beginning your return trip. Expect some congestion (depending on the time of day) as you ride up Route 35 North in the towns of Ortley, Lavallette, and Ocean Beach. Thus, ride with caution. Watch out for cars pulling out of parking spaces and pedestrians heading for the beach.

Continue on Route 35 North through Normandy Beach. Pass the point where Route 35 divides into north and south lanes. Continue into Mantoloking. About a mile north of the Route 35 division is the turn for the Mantoloking Bridge (Route 528) and a traffic light. Make a left here, but do not go over the bridge. Instead, make a sudden right onto Barnegat Lane, a skinny stretch of road that runs parallel with Route 35. Continue along Barnegat Lane to its conclusion about two miles from its origin. In Bay Head Barnegat Lane turns into Clayton Avenue. Follow the road as it bears right onto Johnson Avenue, then make your first left, which is not more than 200 feet away.

You are now on Lake Avenue. Ride up Lake Avenue and pass the picturesque side streets. You'll see why Bay Head reminds some people of Cape Cod. Its weatherworn cedar-shake beach houses seem transplanted from the windswept Cape. Pass through the Bridge Avenue intersection where Bay Head's small cluster of shops is located. Continue on Lake Avenue. On your left will be Twilight Lake. Three streets to your right is the ocean.

Lake Avenue ends at Osborne Avenue. Make a right onto Osborne and then a left at the traffic light back onto Route 35 North. At the next traffic light approximately 200 yards away, bear right. You'll now be on Ocean Avenue in Point Pleasant Beach again. Ride up Ocean Avenue all the way back to the Manasquan Inlet, about two miles away. This concludes the tour.

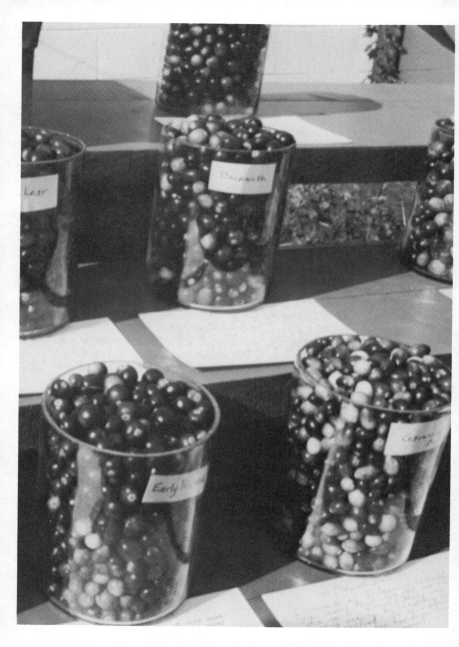

22. Island Beach State Park

County: Ocean
Miles: 16.2
Degree of Difficulty: Easy
Terrain: Flat
Surface: Good
Things to See: Aeolium (Island Beach Nature Center), barrier
  beach landscape, wildlife sanctuary, Barnegat Lighthouse
  ("Old Barney"), Barnegat Inlet

The thin stretch of barrier beach that is Island Beach State Park is, perhaps, the prettiest part of the entire New Jersey Shore. It is made up of miles of unspoiled sandy beaches; delicate, shifting sand dunes; thickets; marshes; and a wildlife sanctuary, home to numerous species of birds including the once endangered osprey. Situated south of Seaside Park with the Atlantic Ocean on one side and Barnegat Bay on the other, Island Beach is the largest undisturbed barrier of its kind in the North Atlantic. And passing right down the center of it, like a spinal cord, is a straight, two-lane road—ideal for cycling.

It is 8.1 miles from the Island Beach State Park entrance at the end of Central Avenue in Seaside Park to where the paved park road ends. Since there is only one road, this tour is a simple down-and-back one. Still, there is much to see in the way of barrier-beach vegetation and birdlife. Do remember to pack binoculars. Island Beach State Park, like Sandy Hook to the north, is located on the Atlantic Flyway, so you'll almost always spot plenty of birds along the tour, especially in the fall.

If you decide to tour Island Beach in the summer or early fall, bring your bathing suit. There are a number of beach access paths along the tour. Feel free to break up your ride with a refreshing ocean dip. Most swimming areas have showers and changing areas, so you won't have to ride in wet swimsuits.

Island Beach State Park is divided into three zones. The northern third of the park is a state natural area. The central third is a

N

How To Get There: Garden State Parkway, Exit 82, to Route 37 East. Follow signs to Island Beach State Park. Route 37 will flow into Central Avenue in Seaside Park. Follow Central Avenue to entrance of park.

ISLAND BEACH STATE PARK: DIRECTIONS AT A GLANCE

1. Follow the one and only park road, from the entrance to the southern tip of the park, and back again.

recreation zone. And the southern third is also a natural area; it includes the park's wildlife sanctuary.

From the park's entrance to the Aeolium or Island Beach Nature Center, it is a little over a mile. Stop here to view the slide show, which will give you a brief overview of barrier beach ecology and the history of Island Beach State Park. View, too, the small nature exhibits there. Also, pick up free brochures that describe vegetation you'll pass along the way and birds you might see in it or just above it.

If you have the time or inclination, walk the short nature trail that begins adjacent to the Aeolium. It offers an "on-site" opportunity to examine up-close barrier beach vegetation. But be forewarned: poison ivy is common at Island Beach, and the mosquitos can be bothersome.

After visiting the Aeolium, continue riding south into the park. The bike path/shoulder you're on, though, ends three miles later. Those who prefer not to ride to the end of the paved road should turn around here. The total mileage for this abbreviated tour is eight miles. Those who proceed should ride to the right and obey traffic laws.

Proceed south to the end of the paved road. There are no turn-offs, bends, or shortcuts. When you arrive at your destination some four miles later, lock your bike and walk to the beach. More ambitious tourists might walk along the beach the mile and a half to Barnegat Inlet.

At one time Island Beach ended where the paved road ends, but because of almost a century of currents and storms, a stretch of sand more than a mile long has built up at the southern end of the peninsula.

Just across the Inlet that separates Island Beach State Park from Long Beach Island is "Old Barney," one of the most photographed and painted lighthouses in all America. After enjoying the view, walk back to your bike and start your return journey.

Island Beach can get windy in late afternoon. Fortunately, the prevailing wind is generally southerly—which means a good tailwind for your return trip. If it's a headwind you face, use the drafting technique described in the "Basics of Bicycle Touring" section of this book. Of course, in order to draft you need at least two riders. If you're alone, you're out of luck.

Some other helpful hints when touring Island Beach State Park: If you're as much a bird-watcher as you are a bicyclist, the best time of the day to tour Island Beach is early morning or dusk, since park birds are most active then. Those who sunburn easily should wear sunscreen if touring in the summer. The sun can be strong, and there are few shady spots along the road. Summer weekends at Island Beach usually mean crowds and traffic. Avoid touring on Saturdays and Sundays if you can. Finally, if you plan to walk any nature trails or partake in any ranger-led activities in the brush, bring insect repellent.

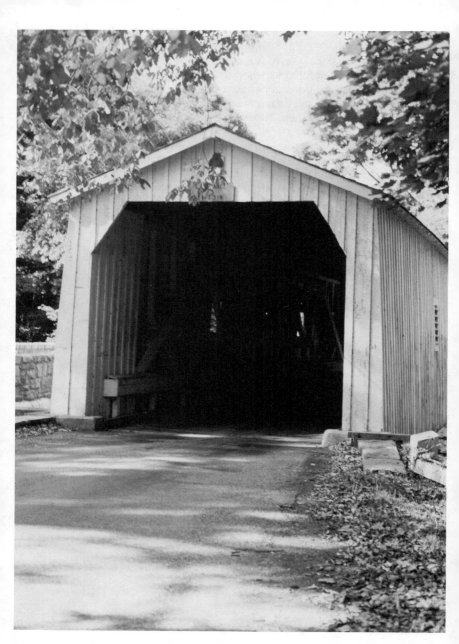

23. Long Beach Island North Loop

County: Ocean
Number of Miles: 18
Degree of Difficulty: Easy
Terrain: Flat
Surface: Good
Things to See: Barnegat Light Historical Museum, Barnegat
Light State Park, "Old Barney," the lighthouse, Viking Village,
views of Barnegat fishing fleet, Barnegat Bay and Barnegat
Inlet

Long Beach Island is one of the Jersey Shore's most popular vacation spots. A skinny stretch of barrier island four miles off Ocean County's coast, Long Beach Island has beautiful beaches, rows of well-kept summer cottages, and a history that includes the settlement of New England whalers and the formation of a prosperous eighteenth-century whaling industry.

Today, Long Beach Island's main industry is summer tourism. Although there is a small year-round population on the island, the towns that make up Long Beach Island just about close up during the winter months. In the winter, cold winds blow hard and frequently, and the sea is rough and choppy. But in the summer and fall Long Beach Island is one of the best places in all of New Jersey for sun, sand, and surf.

Obviously, the best time to tour Long Beach Island is in the summer or early fall. (During the spring, the winds are still fairly strong.) Long Beach Island is eighteen miles long, from the southern tip of the Holgate Division of the Brigantine Wildlife Refuge Area to the northern-most point of Barnegat Light State Park. The width of the island is about a mile and a half at its widest point.

Because a grand loop tour of Long Beach Island would add up to at least thirty-six miles—hardly a "short" bike tour, especially when one takes into account the various stops and things to see— I've broken up the island tour into a North Loop and South Loop.

Both tours originate in Ship Bottom, the centermost town on Long Beach Island and the town in which the Route 72 East Cause-

BROADWAY

Barnegat Light
State Park

Viking Village

BAY VIEW AVE. ST.
20TH. ST.

30TH.
ST.

N

BARNEGAT BAY

LONG BEACH BLVD.

ATLANTIC OCEAN

CENTRAL AVE.
12TH.
ST.

W. 9TH. ST.
START
STOP

How To Get There: Garden State Parkway, Exit 63, to Route 72 East. Route 72 East to Long Beach Island and town of Ship Bottom.

LONG BEACH ISLAND NORTH LOOP: DIRECTIONS AT A GLANCE

1. North on Long Beach Boulevard from 8th Street intersection.
2. Pass through Ship Bottom, Surf City, North Beach, Harvey Cedars, Loveladies, and Barnegat Light. (Long Beach Boulevard becomes Central Avenue in Barnegat Light.)
3. Bear left onto 4th Street.
4. Right at stop sign (Broadway).
5. Right into entrance of Barnegat Light State Park.
6. Left out entrance of Barnegat Light State Park. Proceed on Broadway to 8th Street in Barnegat Light.
7. Right onto 8th Street.
8. Left onto Bay View Avenue.
9. Left onto 30th Street.
10. Right onto Long Beach Boulevard.
11. Long Beach Boulevard to intersection of 24th Street in Surf City.
12. Right onto 24th Street.
13. Left onto Central Avenue.
14. Left onto West 9th Street in Ship Bottom.
15. Left onto Long Beach Boulevard to East 8th Street.

way ends. However, if you're vacationing on the island and wish to complete one (or both) of these tours, you can start anywhere on the loop.

During the summer, the best time to tour Long Beach Island is on a weekday. On weekends traffic is heavy. However, the tour roads are wide and there are well-maintained shoulders on most of them, so if you do choose a weekend to tour the island, you'll still be able to enjoy your ride.

The North Loop tour begins at the intersection of East 8th Street and Long Beach Boulevard in Ship Bottom. East 8th Street runs width-wise and connects with the Route 72 Causeway, a half mile away. Long Beach Boulevard is one of the island's main arteries. It runs the length of Long Beach Island, although it also goes by the name Bay Avenue in Beach Haven, Central Avenue in Barnegat Light, and Route 607 on official state maps.

Proceed north on Long Beach Boulevard through Ship Bottom and then Surf City. These are two densely populated beach towns in the summer, so traffic may be a bit heavy here. Beware of cars pulling in and out of parking spaces and bathers walking to and from the beach. Beyond Surf City, traffic becomes notably lighter.

Continue on Long Beach Boulevard through the towns of North Beach, Harvey Cedars, and Loveladies. Yes, the latter two names are really the names of these communities. Back in the 1700s there actually were cedar trees on this part of the island. As for "Harvey," the town was originally known as Harvey's Whaling Station. Loveladies was named after a local hunter, Thomas Lovelady.

Loveladies is known today for its outstanding collection of contemporary beach homes. Back in 1962 a severe winter storm destroyed most of Loveladies. Homes were washed away by pounding waves and flooding. Property damage ran in the millions. The devastation didn't discourage homeowners from rebuilding, however. What went up were magnificent beach homes with the latest in contemporary architectural design. And all the new homes were constructed on pilings—for protection from further storms and flooding. You'll see these homes on both sides of Long Beach Boulevard.

After Loveladies comes the town of Barnegat Light. Long Beach Boulevard becomes Central Avenue here. At the corner of

5th and Central avenues you'll come to the Barnegat Light Historical Museum, your first stop. The museum is in a former one-room schoolhouse. It contains a number of relics and old photographs from Barnegat Light's Victorian era as well as the original lens of "Old Barney," Barnegat Light's famous lighthouse and namesake, your next stop.

After visiting the museum, stroll through the Edith Duff Gwinn Gardens, located behind the museum. *Note:* The museum has a limited schedule, even in the summer. Check with the Long Beach Island Information Center in Ship Bottom, (609) 499–3407, to find out what days the museum is open.

Leave the museum and continue on Central Avenue to the bend, a street away. Bear left. You're now on 4th Street. At the stop sign on Broadway, make a right. A hundred yards or so on your right is the entrance to Barnegat Light State Park, home of Old Barney, the lighthouse. In front of you is Barnegat Inlet. The land beyond the inlet is Island Beach State Park. (See the Island Beach State Park tour described earlier.)

It is said that Old Barney is the most photographed and painted lighthouse in America; it's one of the few that visitors are still allowed to enter. Climb to the top and you'll have a spectacular bird's-eye view of the Jersey coast.

Barnegat Light State Park is a good place to take a swim should you want to cool off. There are showers here and a place to change clothes. Other than swim and visit Old Barney, there is little to do in this, New Jersey's smallest state park. Make a left out the entrance/exit of the park, and proceed down Broadway to 8th Street.

Make a right on 8th Street and go down to Bay View Avenue where you'll make a left. As you ride down Bay View, you'll get a good glimpse of Barnegat Light's fishing fleet and Barnegat Bay on your right. At the intersection of Bay View and 19th Street, make a right into Viking Village. In the little shacks and shanties, you'll find nautical nicknacks for sale as well as paintings by local artists and handmade gifts.

Continue on Bay View until it ends at 30th Street. Make a left here and go to the stop sign where you'll make a right. You're now back on Long Beach Boulevard. Continue south on Long Beach

Boulevard back through Loveladies, Harvey Cedars, and North Beach.

At the intersection of 24th Street and Long Beach Boulevard in Surf City, make a right. Shortly thereafter, at the yield sign, make a left onto Central Avenue (not the same Central Avenue as the one in Barnegat Light). Follow Central Avenue south toward the Route 72 Causeway.

Pass through Surf City. In Ship Bottom make a left onto West 9th Street. Ride one block and make a left onto Long Beach Boulevard to East 8th Street where the tour began.

24. Long Beach Island South Loop

County: Ocean
Number of Miles: 14.1
Degree of Difficulty: Easy
Terrain: Flat
Surface: Good
Things to See: Bay Village, Fantasy Island, Surflight Theater,
   Long Beach Island Historical Museum

The South Loop tour of Long Beach Island takes in the bottom half of the island. You'll pass through the towns of Ship Bottom, Brant Beach, and Beach Haven. Unlike the North Loop tour, you won't ride to the tip of this part of the island. The very bottom of Long Beach Island is the property of the Brigantine National Wildlife Refuge. Called the Holgate Unit, this wide stretch of beach is good for birdwatching, beach strolling, and surfing—but not bicycling. The reason? There are no roads or pathways, just sand. Holgate is, nonetheless, worth spending some time in, even if it's for a walk along the beach. Just don't plan on taking your bike with you.

The South Loop tour begins in Ship Bottom at the intersection of Central Avenue and West 9th Street. Proceed down Central Avenue to West 28th Street, where you must make a left. Ride up to the intersection with Long Beach Boulevard and turn right. Proceed down the boulevard, which runs the length of the island, to Beach Haven. Along the way you'll pass stores that sell beach paraphernalia and nautical nicknacks, surf shops and boutiques that cater to the summer tourist.

It is a good four or five miles to Beach Haven, South Long Beach Island's most popular tourist town. Once you get into Beach Haven, you'll come across Bay Village, the island's biggest shopping mall. Next to that is the Thundering Surf Water Slide, the source of great fun and excitement when the waves are flat and the beach is boring. Finally, there is Fantasy Island, Long Beach Island's only amusement park.

After you pass these sites, you'll come to Engleside Avenue, a main thoroughfare to the beach, just a couple of blocks away. Make

How To Get There: Garden State Parkway, Exit 63, to Route 72 East. Route 72 East to Long Beach Island and town of Ship Bottom.

LONG BEACH ISLAND SOUTH LOOP: DIRECTIONS AT A GLANCE

1. South onto Central Avenue in Ship Bottom to West 28th Street.
2. Left onto West 28th Street.
3. Right onto Long Beach Boulevard.
4. Left onto Engleside Avenue in Beach Haven.
5. Left onto Atlantic Avenue.
6. Left at the conclusion of Atlantic Avenue.
7. Right back onto Long Beach Boulevard.
8. Left onto 9th Street in Ship Bottom.
9. Tour ends at intersection of 9th Street and Central Avenue in Ship Bottom.

a left onto Engleside. You are now in Beach Haven's historic district. Although the resort doesn't have the reputation or charm of either Cape May or Ocean Grove, Beach Haven does have its share of interesting Victorian summer homes, many of which have been restored.

Ride up to the Long Beach Island Historical Museum located on the corner of Engleside and Atlantic avenues. Here you can pick up a walking tour brochure and view the most interesting of the Victorian homes within a three- or four-block radius of the museum.

Even if you decide against the walking tour, do plan to spend some time in the museum. It is one of the better small museums in southern New Jersey. Inside the former church, now the home of the Long Beach Island Historical Society, you'll see displays that depict the island's importance as a whaling center and photos of the now infamous March 1962 storm that devastated the island and caused millions of dollars in property damage.

Directly across the street from the museum is the Surflight Theater, a popular nightspot for island vacationers. Here drama students, up and coming New York actors and actresses, and even veteran players from the regional theater circuit star in a full season of mostly musicals and comedies. Across from both the theater and museum is the Beach Haven Band Shell and adjoining field where free concerts occur weekly throughout the summer.

After your museum visit, ride one block east (toward the ocean) on Engleside Avenue to Atlantic Avenue. Make a left onto Atlantic Avenue and begin your ride back to Ship Bottom. Notice that there is a designated bicycle lane on Atlantic Avenue. Ride in it and you'll stay out of the way of passing cars. Beware of pedestrians, though. Beach-goers must cross Atlantic Avenue to get to the sand and surf.

Continue along Atlantic Avenue to its end, where you'll make a left and two blocks later, a right back onto Long Beach Boulevard. Ride north on the boulevard through Brant Beach and Ship Bottom to 9th Street in the latter town. Here, make a left and return to your starting point on 9th Street and Central Avenue.

25. The Pine Barrens

County: Burlington
Number of Miles: 25
Degree of Difficulty: Easy
Terrain: Flat
Surface: Good
Things to See: Wharton State Forest, Batsto Village and the
    Richards' Mansion, Mullica River, Wading River, Pine Barrens
    forest

The Pine Barrens cover nearly one-fourth of New Jersey. Located
smack in the middle of the state, this remarkable wilderness area is
home to fifty-four threatened plant species and thirty-five threatened wildlife species. Underneath this vast area of pitch pine forest,
cedar swamps, marshlands, and tea-colored rivers is the Cohansey
Aquifer, a huge, seventeen-trillion-gallon lake. It's possible that the
lake contains the purest water in America.

Much of the Pine Barrens is under federal and state protection
from development and land abuse. The area is sparsely settled, and
the towns found in the heart of the Pines are hardly towns at all
anymore. Most contain few residents—and even fewer buildings.
Some are actual ghost towns. Because of the lack of people in the
Pines, there are very few paved roads. Those roads are ideal for
bicycle riding, though, and two-wheel touring is a great way to
experience the Pine Barrens.

Begin your ride in the Batsto Village parking area, just off
Route 542. Part of Wharton State Forest, Batsto Village is a nineteenth century bog-iron community that today features a number
of restored buildings including a general store, post office, gristmill,
threshing barn, workers' homes, and the Richards' Mansion, a
beautiful and interesting structure once owned by bog-iron baron
Jesse Richards.

Take time to stroll around Batsto Village before or after your
Pine Barrens bicycle tour. Special events are frequently held at Batsto during the summer and fall. Call (609) 561–0024 for details.

How To Get There: Garden State Parkway to Route 542 West to Wharton State Forest and Batsto Village. Follow signs on Route 542 to Batsto.

THE PINE BARRENS: DIRECTIONS AT A GLANCE

1. Left onto Route 542 out of the Batsto Village parking lot.
2. Left onto Route 563.
3. Right at the intersection of Route 563 and Route 679 (also known as the Route 563 Spur).
4. Right at the Union Hill Campground intersection stop sign.
5. Right at stop sign. Proceed to Route 542.
6. Route 542 to Batsto Village.

Also, be certain to stop at the Visitor's Center where you can purchase books and pamphlets about the cultural and natural history of the Pine Barrens. There are a number of fine exhibits in the Visitor's Center mini-museum; these will give you a clear picture of the importance of not only Batsto, but the entire Pine Barrens over the past two hundred years.

Start your tour by making a left onto Route 542 and heading east. Some two miles later you'll pass a wide section of the Mullica River, one of the Pine Barrens' best canoeing rivers. Continue east on Route 542. Notice the occasional vacant home. Almost all the derelict homes you pass were built at the turn of the century or before. Despite their shoddy state, they are fine examples of the Victorian-influenced Pine Barrens' architecture of that period.

Make a left onto Route 563 and head north. The next five miles will be through Wharton State Forest. Notice the scrub pine and pitch pine trees on both sides of you. You'll pass a gun club or two, but little else in the way of buildings or people. Traffic will be light, except, perhaps, on weekends and holidays.

Make a right at the intersection of Route 563 and Route 679 (also known as the Route 563 Spur). Route 679 won't be marked; look for the stop sign and turn there. Heading south now, you'll pass Harrisville Lake, Bodine Field (a major camping area in Wharton State Forest), and more wooded area.

Make a right at the Union Hill Campground intersection. Follow signs for Batsto Village and Route 542. At the next stop sign, make a right and proceed to Route 542, heading west toward Batsto. Cross over the Wading River, another prime Pine Barrens canoeing river. You are now back on Route 542. Follow it to Batsto Village where the tour concludes.

26. The Lumberton–Vincentown Loop

County: Burlington
Number of Miles: 25
Degree of Difficulty: Easy
Terrain: Flat
Surface: Fair
Things to See: Lumberton, Vincentown, South Jersey farmland,
Pine Barrens

Lumberton is a small, sleepy town on the outskirts of the Pine Barrens. Located just south of Mount Holly and Rancocas State Park, Lumberton used to be a thriving river town when barges on Rancocas Creek would bring goods made in Lumberton out to the Delaware River and Philadelphia.

The Lumberton-Vincentown Loop begins in the parking lot of the Ridgeway A. Gaun Community Center on Route 541, also called the Lumberton-Mount Holly Road, the town's main artery. Get permission to park in the lot, or park on a side street nearby. Make a left out of the lot onto Route 541 and ride a couple blocks to Landing Street. Make a left onto Landing. A quarter mile later you'll come to a fork in the road. Stay straight. You'll now be on Municipal Drive. (If you went right at the fork, you'd stay on Landing Street.)

Proceed on Municipal Drive. Pass through the stop sign intersection. Municipal Drive now becomes Newbolds Corner Road. You'll now be in South Jersey countryside where sod, horse, and dairy farms sit alongside modern housing developments.

At the next stop sign, some four miles later, make a right onto Vincentown-Columbus Road. This road will lead you onto Main Street in Vincentown. While Lumberton has remained a quiet residential town, Vincentown is beginning to attract occasional antique hunters and general store lovers. In these charming shops, and wonderfully restored turn-of-the-century homes, you will find the atmosphere of America's Victorian era carefully preserved.

How To Get There: Route 295 to Route 38 (toward Mount Holly). Route 38 to Route 541 (Lumberton-Mount Holly Road) to Ridgeway A. Gaun Community Center in Lumberton.

LUMBERTON-VINCENTOWN LOOP: DIRECTIONS AT A GLANCE

1. Left onto Route 541, out Ridgeway A. Gaun Community Center parking lot.
2. Left onto Landing Street.
3. At the fork, stay straight. You're now on Municipal Drive. (Municipal Drive eventually becomes Newbolds Corner Road.)
4. Right onto Vincentown-Columbus Road. This road eventually becomes Main Street in Vincentown. Cross over Route 206. Main Street becomes Retreat Road.
5. At the "Y" intersection of Retreat Road and Big Hill Road, bear right onto Big Hill Road.
6. Big Hill Road turns into Vincentown-South Park Road (also called Sooy Place Road) after crossing over Route 70.
7. Right on Powell Place Road. (Powell Place Road has two links with Sooy Place. Your right hand turn is the *second* one.)
8. Right onto New Road.
9. Right onto Ridge Road.
10. Left onto Isaac-Budd Road, also known as Buddtown Road.
11. Right onto Main Street in Vincentown.
12. Left onto Mill Street.
13. At the fork, right onto Landing Street.
14. Left onto Municipal Drive in Lumberton.
15. Right onto Route 541.
16. Follow Route 541 through Lumberton to Ridgeway A. Gaun Community Center.

Vincentown–Columbus Road becomes Main Street in the town of Vincentown. Cross over Route 206. Main Street becomes Retreat Road. Follow Retreat Road to the "Y" intersection. Bear right onto Big Hill Road. Follow Big Hill Road to the Route 70 intersection. On the other side of Route 70 Big Hill Road turns into Vincentown-South Park Road—according to county maps. But, the street sign at the intersection indicates the road is called Sooy Place Road.

You'll notice that the scenery on Sooy Place Road is much different than the scenery outside of Lumberton. You are now in the Pine Barrens. You'll pass pitch pine forest and cranberry bogs as well as recently-built small housing developments.

Continue on Sooy Place Road to the Powell Place Road intersection where the old Pine Tavern used to be (see historic marker at intersection) and a picturesque horse farm still sits. (*Note:* Powell Place Road has two links with Sooy Place. Your right hand turn is the *second* one.) Make a hard right onto Powell Place Road. (Although I've been told this road will eventually be paved, at press time it was still unpaved.) Follow Powell Place Road through the Pine Barrens town of Tabernacle. Notice how developers are slowly but surely creeping into the Pines. Off Powell Road are new side streets with new homes on them. Fifteen years ago this whole area was virgin forest.

Continue on Powell Place Road. At the New Road intersection and stop sign, make a right. Proceed on New Road and cross Route 70, about a mile or two away. Continue on New Road to the Ridge Road intersection. There is a four-way stop sign intersection here. Make a right onto Ridge Road and proceed to Isaac-Budd Road, passing the Retreat Road stop sign intersection. Make a left onto Isaac-Budd Road, also known as Buddtown Road. You'll pass more sod and horse farms as you're now out of the Pine Barrens.

Cross over Route 206 and go to the Main Street stop sign, about a quarter mile from Route 206. Make a right onto Main Street. You're back in Vincentown. This is the same Main Street you rode on earlier in the tour. Proceed back into the center of Vincentown, but this time, make a left onto Mill Street instead of backtracking on Vincentown-Columbus Road.

A half mile from the Main Street-Mill Street intersection you'll come to something of a fork intersection. Make a right onto Landing Street. (If you went left, you'd be on Route 616.)

Three miles down Landing Street you'll come to a stop sign intersection. Pass through the intersection. Follow Landing Street to its end where you'll make a left onto Municipal Drive in Lumberton. A quarter mile farther is the Route 541 intersection. Make a right here and ride back to the Ridgeway A. Gaun Community Center where the tour concludes.

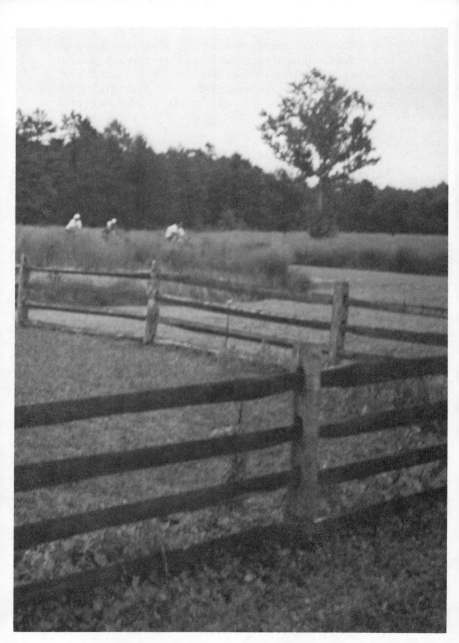

27. The Jersey Devil Run

County: Atlantic
Number of Miles: 10.2
Degree of Difficulty: Easy
Terrain: Flat
Surface: Good
Things to See: Smithville (shops, boutiques, Tomasello Winery,
  Smithville Inn), Noyes Museum, Leed's Point

Located on the fringe of the Pine Barrens a few miles north of Atlantic
City, the "Historic Towne of Smithville" is a popular South Jersey
tourist attraction. More than thirty boutiques, shops, and restaurants
comprise the town that sits on the banks of Lake Meone. Many of the
buildings were constructed in the eighteenth and nineteenth centu-
ries and were carefully moved to Smithville from other locations in
the Pine Barrens. The remaining buildings in the town are colonial
replicas.

The Smithville Inn, built two hundred years ago, is a popular
restaurant. Back in colonial times the Baremore family catered to
hungry and tired stagecoach travelers. The Inn was a working establishment until the early 1900s when it was abandoned and fell
into disrepair. However, in 1949, the Noyes family purchased the
Inn and restored its original charm and usefulness. Other historic
buildings were later purchased and relocated near the Smithville
Inn. Gradually, merchants moved in, and Smithville began to lure
tourists.

Before embarking on your tour of the Smithville-Leed's Point
area, stroll through Smithville. Visit the old mill (now an antique
shop) where a large water wheel is still capable of turning water
from Lake Meone. If you're a wine lover, pay a visit to the Tomasello Winery where you'll be able to sample some nineteen wines
and seven champagnes, all made with grapes grown in New Jersey
vineyards.   Also on display are pieces of antique wine-making
equipment. Other shops sell antique reproduction furniture, clothes,
colonial bric-a-brac, and Pine Barrens folk art. Perhaps make reser-

153

Smithville

Inn

RTE. #561

Cemetery

RTE. #561

Parking Lot

MOSS MILL RD.

Blinker

START/STOP

SMITHVILLE BLVD

RTE. #9

LEED'S POINT RD. (RTE. #618)

(RTE. #634) PITNEY RD.

Stop Sign

Brigantine Ntl. Wildlife Refuge

Noyes Museum

Stop Sign

GREAT CREEK RD.

N

How To Get There: Garden State Parkway to Route 9. Turn onto Route 561 in Oceanville. Smithville is located at intersection of Route 9 and 561.

THE JERSEY DEVIL RUN: DIRECTIONS AT A GLANCE

1. Right onto Route 561 (out of the Smithville parking lot).
2. Cross Route 9.
3. Right onto Leed's Point Road (Route 618).
4. Left onto Route 9.
5. Left onto Great Creek Road.
6. Right onto Noyes Museum dirt road.
7. Right onto Route 9.
8. Left onto Great Creek Road.
9. Right onto Pitney Road (Route 634).
10. Right onto Moss Mill Road (Route 561).
11. Moss Mill Road becomes Smithville Boulevard. Left at Smithville Boulevard–Route 9 intersection.
12. Left at Route 9–Route 561 intersection to Smithville parking lot.

vations before you go for a meal at the Smithville Inn upon your return.

The tour begins in the Smithville parking lot located on Route 561, just across from the shops. Make a right out of the parking lot and onto Route 561. Two hundred yards later, you'll come upon a stop sign and the Route 9 intersection. Cross Route 9 and head toward Leed's Point. Notice the old cemetery to your right. Many tombstones date back to the eighteenth century. Continue on Route 561.

Approximately one and a half miles later, you'll come to Leed's Point Road (Route 618). Make a right here. This area is rich in New Jersey folklore. According to legend, this is where the infamous Jersey Devil was born.

The way some locals tell it, the horned, winged creature, with the face of a horse and the tail of a demon, was the result of an illicit affair between a certain Mrs. Leeds and a young, handsome British army officer around the time of the Revolutionary War. Others swear a curse fell upon the demon because he was the thirteenth child of poor Mrs. Leeds. In any event, shortly after his birth the creature flew out of an open window and has terrified the countryside ever since . . . or so legend has it.

Continue south on Route 618 until the stop sign at the Route 9 intersection. Make a left onto Route 9. Proceed for not more than a fifth of a mile, at which point you'll come to the Great Creek Road intersection. Make a left onto Great Creek Road, and follow signs for Brigantine National Wildlife Refuge, also called the Edwin B. Forsythe National Wildlife Refuge.

For those who would like to combine the Brigantine National Wildlife Refuge Tour (see page **159**) with this tour, continue to the entrance of the refuge. If you, however, prefer to bicycle Brigantine's dirt road loop at another time, turn right off Great Creek Road and onto the dirt road where the Noyes Museum is located. There will be a sign that identifies the dirt road and an entrance to the Noyes Museum property just after the bend in Great Creek Road. Proceed approximately two hundred yards up the dirt road. On your right will be the museum and parking area.

The same family which purchased and restored the Smithville Inn also financed the construction of this fine arts museum.

Opened in 1983, the Noyes Museum is now Southern New Jersey's largest art museum, and a visit to it is highly recommended. Of particular interest is the museum's collection of waterfowl and shore bird decoys. Fred Noyes was once a serious collector of such decoys. Many of his most prized decoys are now on exhibit in the museum.

The museum also has other exhibits on display. They often feature the work of noted New Jersey sculptors, painters, and furniture makers. The museum, however, is not open every day. For information on when it is open, as well as information on current exhibits and special programs, call (609) 652–8848.

Make a right out of the Noyes Museum parking lot and go in the opposite direction from which you came. At the stop sign, which is the Route 9 intersection, make a right and proceed to Great Creek Road, approximately one-tenth of a mile north. Make a left onto Great Creek Road. (If you went right, you'd head back toward the Brigantine National Wildlife Refuge and the entrance to the Noyes Museum.)

Continue on Great Creek Road. It is a long stretch of road, flat and smooth, and perfect for hitting an "energetic" riding pace. At the next stop sign, make a right onto Pitney Road (Route 634). Proceed to the blinking light, which is the intersection of Pitney Road and Moss Mill Road (Route 561). Bear right where Moss Mill Road becomes Smithville Boulevard. Follow Smithville Boulevard to the stop sign intersection. Smithville Boulevard meets Route 9 here. Make a left onto Route 9. A mile or so down Route 9, you'll come to the Route 561 intersection. Make a left here and ride to the Smithville parking lot where the tour originates.

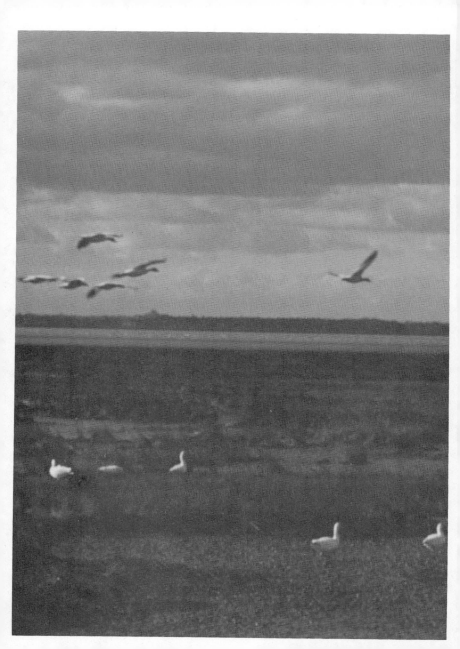

28. Brigantine National Wildlife Refuge

County: Atlantic
Number of Miles: 8.5
Degree of Difficulty: Moderate
Terrain: Flat
Surface: Rough (dirt road)
Things to See: Visitor's Center, Wildlife Refuge, Atlantic City
skyline, marshland, Great Bay, Reed's Bay, birds

Talk about birds! More than 250 species of them visit the Brigantine National Wildlife Refuge, also known as the Edwin B. Forsythe National Wildlife Refuge, each year. You don't have to be an avid bird watcher to appreciate this beautiful bird refuge. There are birds near the water, on the water, in the marshland, and in the sky above the Refuge. They squeak, squawk, and sing. Such sights and sounds make this tour a truly special one.

But there is a catch. The eight-and-a-half-mile Refuge loop road is not paved. It is kept in good condition by rangers, but it is a dirt road. Thus, an all-terrain or mountain bike is recommended for this tour. That is not to say, however, one couldn't complete the tour on a standard ten-speed or even a three-speed. It has been done. But riding one of these bikes will mean a rough ride, and the tour certainly won't be as enjoyable for you as it would be for those pedaling bikes equipped with fat tires.

Most people who visit the Brigantine National Wildlife Refuge do so by car. In fact, at the Visitor's Center a self-guided "Auto Tour" of the refuge is available to visitors. Pick up one of these free pamphlets and use it as any driver would.

Be sure to spend some time at the Visitor's Center before you embark on your bike tour. The wildlife exhibits are informative, and the many different slide shows that rangers show in the auditorium are especially stimulating. Also, pick up another pamphlet called "Birds of Edwin B. Forsythe National Wildlife Refuge." It contains a bird checklist so you can keep track of your personal sightings, if you desire. It also contains information on what season you're

159

GREAT CREEK RD.

RTE. #9

LILY LAKE RD.

START STOP

Visitor's Ctr.

N

Observation Tower

Observation Tower

Marsh

How To Get There: Garden State Parkway to Route 9 in Oceanville. Follow signs to Brigantine National Wildlife Refuge (also called Edwin B. Forsythe National Wildlife Refuge). Turn onto Great Creek Road. Follow Great Creek Road to the entrance of the Wildlife Refuge.

BRIGANTINE NATIONAL WILDLIFE REFUGE: DIRECTIONS AT A GLANCE

1. Follow the dirt road loop around the Refuge.
2. At its conclusion, make a left onto Great Creek Road and ride back to the Visitor's Center parking area.

most apt to see what bird, plus the average number of yearly sightings. Having this kind of information at your disposal only makes the tour more rewarding.

Begin your tour at the entrance of the dirt road loop. The only directions you need are to follow the loop. However, the unpaved road will ultimately end in a location other than where you began. You will notice that the dirt road ends on Great Creek Road—the road you took to get to the Refuge. Simply turn left onto Great Creek Road and ride back to the Visitor's Center where you began your tour and probably parked your car. The distance is not more than a mile.

While on the loop road, you'll notice that there are fourteen numbered "stops." These correspond to information contained in the "Auto Tour" brochure. Serious bird watcher/bicyclists can easily spend a morning or afternoon admiring the birds and beauty of the Refuge. Binoculars are recommended, but they are not mandatory to enjoy your outing. Insect repellent, however, is a good idea. Mosquitos and green head flies can be a nuisance.

On the loop road you'll get a superb view of the Atlantic City skyline to the south. The body of water that separates Atlantic City and the Refuge is Reed's Bay. The bay on the northern side of the Refuge is known as Great Bay.

Like most of the Jersey Shore marshland and protected natural area tours included in this book, the Brigantine National Wildlife Refuge is located on the Atlantic Flyway. Because of Brigantine's location, a large variety and number of birds use it as a migratory stop-off. The best time to bike the loop road and view the birds is during autumn when many birds are migrating south. Dawn and dusk are better than late morning and afternoon, since birds are most active then. Those most interested in ducks and geese will want to bicycle the route in November. It will be a bit chilly perhaps, but the thousands of ducks and Canadian geese that pack the refuge that month make this small discomfort worthwhile.

29. Victorian Cape May

County: Cape May
Number of Miles: 8.3
Degree of Difficulty: Easy
Terrain: Flat
Surface: Good
Things to See: Cape May Welcome Center, Washington Street
    Mall, beach area, Cape May historic district, Cape May
    County Art League Museum, Emlen Physick Estate and
    Mansion

The best way to see and experience the Victorian splendor of Cape May is by bicycle. You'll agree the moment you arrive. Parking is a big problem; the streets are narrow, and spaces are at a premium since Cape May's founding fathers never considered the possibility of the horseless carriage. Once you do find a parking space—and you will if you arrive early—you'll not want to move your car until it's time to leave.

There is another reason why a tour of Victorian Cape May is best by bike. Cape May is a compact town; you can almost see it all by foot. But that's time-consuming and taxing. On a bike, you'll see the entire town and all its architectural delights, stopping where you wish to stop, and leisurely pedaling on to your next destination.

This is an easy tour, a family tour. The mileage is low, the terrain flat, and because you'll spend most of your time on narrow, tree-lined streets, the pace has to be slow. You don't even need to bring your own bike. There are a number of bike shops in Cape May that rent three-speeds and even tandems for a modest fee.

Cape May, of course, is one of New Jersey's most popular tourist destinations. Each year thousands of people visit Cape May to enjoy its vast Victorian heritage, eat at its many acclaimed restaurants, shop, spend a day at the beach, or overnight at one of the town's internationally-known bed & breakfasts. And, organizations like the Mid-Atlantic Center for the Arts and the Cape May Chamber

How To Get There: Garden State Parkway, Exit 1.
Follow signs to Cape May.

VICTORIAN CAPE MAY: DIRECTIONS AT A GLANCE

1. From the Welcome Center parking lot, left onto Lafayette Street.
2. Right onto Ocean Street.
3. Left onto Beach Drive (also known as Beach Avenue).
4. Round the Wilmington Street bend at the end of Beach Drive.
5. Left at stop sign onto New Jersey Avenue.
6. Right onto Pittsburgh Avenue, which eventually turns into Texas Avenue.
7. Bear to the right at the Texas Avenue–Washington Street intersection.
8. Follow the bend to Lafayette Street. Left on Lafayette.
9. Left onto Sidney Street.
10. Right onto Washington Street.
11. Left onto Madison Avenue.
12. Right onto Stockton Avenue.
13. Right onto Howard Street.
14. Right onto Sewell Avenue.
15. Left onto Franklin Street.
16. Left onto Hughes Street.
17. Left onto Ocean Street.
18. Left onto Columbia Avenue.
19. Right onto Jefferson Street.
20. Right onto Kearney Avenue.
21. Right onto Guerney Street.
22. Left onto Columbia Avenue.
23. Left onto Decatur Street.
24. Right onto Beach Drive.
25. Make a U-turn at the conclusion of Beach Drive, then a left onto Broadway.
26. Right onto West Perry Street.
27. Left onto Lafayette Street.
28. Left into Welcome Center parking lot.

of Commerce do their part to make sure there is always something going on. Cape May is popular with young and old alike; many return again and again.

This tour begins at the Cape May Welcome Center, located on Lafayette Street across from the municipal parking lot. Inside, you'll find all the information on Cape May you'll ever need, including that pertaining to bicycle rentals, restaurants, accommodations, tours, and special events.

Proceed out the small Welcome Center parking lot and make a left onto Lafayette Street. Ride to the traffic light and make a right onto Ocean Street. Two blocks later you'll pass the Washington Street Mall on your right. The mall is Cape May's noted shopping district. Cafes, boutiques, souvenir shops, and restaurants can also be found here.

Continue down Ocean Street to the traffic light at Beach Drive (also called Beach Avenue). Beach Drive runs parallel to the boardwalk and beach, which are directly in front of you. Make a left onto Beach Drive. Pass Cape May's Convention Hall, some boardwalk concession stands, and Victorian beachfront homes. Beach Drive is a busy street, especially during the summer; therefore, ride with caution. Fortunately, traffic lightens considerably once you're out of the Ocean Street area.

Beach Drive concludes at the north end of Cape May. Round the bend onto Wilmington Street. Make a left onto New Jersey Avenue at the stop sign, and ride to Pittsburgh Avenue a few blocks away. Make a right onto Pittsburgh Avenue. This is a good cycling street. It's flat and the shoulders are wide enough for cyclists to ride two abreast if they wish.

Pittsburgh Avenue eventually turns into Texas Avenue. Notice the docks and marina to your right. At the Texas Avenue–Washington Street intersection, bear to your right. (You can't go left; it's a one-way street.) Follow the bend in the road to the Lafayette Street intersection a short distance away. Once again, you'll see the marina and the home of the Cape May commercial fishing fleet.

Make a left onto Lafayette Street and then another left onto Sidney Street which comes up rather quickly. Go to the end of Sidney Street, a hundred yards away, and make a right onto Washington Street. Proceed down Washington Street to the Cape May

County Art League Museum and the Emlen Physick Estate and Mansion, your first two stops.

At the Cape May County Art League Museum you'll find the paintings and sculptures of many of the area's top artists plus special exhibits. The main attraction at the Physick Estate, however, is the sixteen-room mansion built by the renowned architect Frank Furness. Tours of the mansion are popular since its interior has been meticulously restored to its original grandeur and is filled with beautiful Victorian furnishings. The Welcome Center will have a tour schedule should you decide to see the inside of the mansion.

Just after the Physick Estate is Madison Avenue. Make a left here. Pass the Cape May Memorial Park and proceed down Madison to Stockton Avenue, which is one block away from the end of Madison and the beach. Make a right onto Stockton Avenue. (Directly opposite Stockton Avenue, on the left side of Madison Avenue, is New Jersey Avenue.)

Stockton Avenue will lead you to Cape May's historic district. At the conclusion of Stockton Avenue there is a "T" intersection. Make a right onto Howard Street here. You are now in the heart of the historic district as evidenced by the many Victorian homes all around you. Make a right onto Sewell Avenue, a couple of blocks away, and then a left onto Franklin Street. Pass Columbia Avenue and make a left onto Hughes Street, the next one up.

Hughes is called the prettiest street in Cape May. Some have even called it the prettiest residential street in America. Virtually all the homes on Hughes Street have been tastefully restored, and the trees and occasional white picket fence give the street a homey, classic American warmth.

Make a left at the stop sign onto Ocean Street and then another left at the next street down. The turn will put you onto Columbia Avenue, the street with Cape May's two most noted bed & breakfast inns on it. Both the Abbey and the Mainstay have been featured in numerous travel and Americana magazines as well as in many bed & breakfast guidebooks. The interiors of both seem like Victorian museums. Antiques are everywhere. Attention was paid to every detail when the structures were restored. The Abbey will be on your right a hundred yards from the stop sign and across from the war monument in the middle of the street. The Mainstay is on the opposite side of Columbia Avenue, just beyond the monument. Signs hanging off their porches will help identify them.

Continue on Columbia Avenue to Jefferson Street. Make a right onto Jefferson and head in the direction of the beach. At the Kearney Avenue intersection, make a right. Proceed on Kearney Avenue to Guerney Street. Make a right onto Guerney Street and then a left back onto Columbia Avenue. You'll pass the monument again as well as the Abbey.

Cross over Ocean Street and proceed to Decatur Street where you'll make a left. Once again, ride toward the beach, and make a right onto Beach Drive. Pass Congress Hall, which President Benjamin Harrison once used as his summer White House. Ride down to the very end of Beach Drive. Here, you'll have a good view of the Cape May Point Lighthouse.

Make a U-turn and head back on Beach Drive to Broadway, a couple of blocks away. Make a left onto Broadway. At the West Perry Street traffic light, make a right. Follow West Perry as it winds its way to the Lafayette Street intersection. You'll pass Swain's Hardware complex on your left. The small stretch from Swain's to the Lafayette Street intersection can be a little tricky. When in doubt, follow signs for the Parkway.

Make a left onto Lafayette Street and then a left into the Welcome Center parking lot. The tour concludes here.

30. Cape May Point Pedal

County: Cape May
Number of Miles: 9
Degree of Difficulty: Easy
Terrain: Flat
Surface: Good
Things to See: Cape May Bird Refuge, Sunset Beach, USS
  Atlantus, Cape May Point (town), Cape May Point State Park
  (lighthouse, Visitor's Center, Hawkwatch Observation Deck)

The Cape May area has more than Victorian charm to lure bicyclists and other tourists. On the outskirts of the town, and in Cape May Point, there is much to see and do. If you're ambitious or your time is tight, you can combine this tour with the preceding tour of Victorian Cape May. You might do one tour in the morning and the other in the afternoon. But for some cyclists, that will leave time for little else.

The ideal way to explore the Cape May area by bike is to make it a two-day affair. Leisurely tour the town one day, then the next day complete this tour. To set up your bicycle exploration of the Cape May area this way will allow you to spend ample time visiting the sights along the road, rather than simply riding by them. Cape May is really too special a place to try to see it all in one day.

If you decide on a two-day outing, consider staying in one of Cape May's many excellent bed & breakfasts. Advance reservations are almost always a must. Some B&Bs, as they're called, even have bikes for guests' use. Cape May attracts tourists nine months out of the year. Only in January, February, and March is the town not full of tourists. Unfortunately, these months aren't exactly optimum bicycling months in the Garden State.

The best time to tour Cape May is in the fall. September is an excellent month, because the weather is usually warm, not hot, and the summer crowds are gone. October is a good month, too, because Cape May hosts its popular Victorian Week then. There are many special events, including house tours, antique and craft shows, and square dancing contests to enjoy.

How To Get There: Garden State Parkway, Exit 1.
Follow signs to Cape May.

CAPE MAY POINT PEDAL: DIRECTIONS AT A GLANCE

1. Right onto Lafayette Street (out of Welcome Center parking lot).
2. Right at the Perry Street stop sign. Bear left onto West Perry Street.
3. West Perry Street becomes Sunset Boulevard. Ride down Sunset Boulevard to Sunset Beach.
4. Return on Sunset Boulevard to Cape Avenue. Make a right.
5. Proceed around Cape May Point circle and continue on Cape Avenue to Yale Avenue.
6. Left onto Yale Avenue.
7. Enter Cape May Point State Park.
8. Follow park road to lighthouse, Visitor's Center, and Hawkwatch Observation Deck.
9. Exit Cape May Point State Park. Make a right onto Lighthouse Avenue.
10. Right onto Sunset Boulevard.
11. Left onto Bayshore Road (Route 607).
12. Right onto Stimpson Lane.
13. Right onto Seashore Road (Route 626).
14. Seashore Road turns into Broadway. Left onto York Avenue.
15. Right onto Park Boulevard.
16. Left onto West Perry Street.
17. Left onto Lafayette Street.
18. Left into Welcome Center parking lot.

It is Cape May's grand celebration of Victoriana. However, the streets are congested, especially on the weekends, which doesn't make for ideal cycling situations. If you do go to Cape May to bicycle during Victorian Week, make it on a weekday, if possible. That way your cycling experience should be a rewarding one, since there will be fewer cars on the road.

The Cape May Point Pedal begins in the Welcome Center parking lot on Lafayette Street in Cape May. It is the same starting point as for the Victorian Cape May tour. Make a right out of the parking lot onto Lafayette Street. Approximately fifty yards down the road is a stop sign. To the left of the sign is Jackson Street; to the right is Perry Street. Make a right at the stop sign and proceed to the next intersection, which comes up quickly. Bear left here. Swain's Hardware store will be on your right. The brightly painted Bernard-Goode House, a popular bed & breakfast with the best breakfast spread in town, will be on your left.

Perry Street becomes West Perry Street after you pass Swain's Hardware store. Then, once you're beyond the traffic light at the intersection of West Perry and Broadway, West Perry becomes Sunset Boulevard. Head down Sunset. Your destination is Sunset Beach, which is located at the end of Sunset Boulevard, some two miles away.

Along the way you'll pass the Cape May Bird Refuge. Those cyclists interested in bird watching will find a stop here worthwhile. If you are a bird watcher, do pack binoculars. You'll get a chance to use them here and then again in Cape May Point State Park.

Once you arrive at Sunset Beach, find a suitable bicycle parking space and walk to the water. Offshore a few hundred yards you'll notice what looks like a concrete bulkhead of some sort. Actually, it's the remains of the USS *Atlantus*, a 3000-ton concrete freighter built in the waning days of World War I when steel was scarce. The concrete ship experiment was a failure due to the excessive weight and density of such a vessel. In 1926 the *Atlantus* went aground during a storm. Now it's a state historic site.

Sunset Beach is interesting for another reason, too. It is where you can find "Cape May diamonds," quartz crystals that bear a remarkable resemblance to real diamonds. Don't fret if you can't find one; you can purchase all you want in the shops that line the

Sunset Beach parking lot.

After visiting Sunset Beach, backtrack on Sunset Boulevard until you come to Cape Avenue and the entrance to Cape May Point. Make a right onto Cape Avenue and head toward Cape May Point State Park, your next destination.

A few blocks down Cape Avenue is a circle. Bear right around it until you meet up with Cape Avenue again. (It is halfway around the circle.) Proceed down Cape Avenue until the intersection with Yale Avenue. Make a left here. Pass the Cape May Point Post Office on your right. Continue on Yale Avenue to the intersection of Lehigh Avenue. Across from the intersection is the entrance to Cape May Point State Park.

Proceed into the park. On your right is the Cape May Point Lighthouse. Just beyond the lighthouse, bear right and proceed to the Visitor's Center. You'll want to spend some time here. Check out the nature exhibits and familiarize yourself with park activities by way of the many free pamphlets available.

Across from the Visitor's Center is the Hawkwatch Observation Deck. Pedal over and check out the latest hawk sighting tally. Once again, bird watchers might want to spend a bit more time here than non-birders.

Follow the exit signs and leave the park the same way you rode in. At the stop sign make a right onto Lighthouse Avenue. Proceed on Lighthouse Avenue to Sunset Boulevard. Make a right onto Sunset and head back toward Cape May. Pass the Cape May Bird Refuge again, but instead of continuing on Sunset Boulevard, make a left onto Bayshore Road (Route 607).

Proceed on Bayshore Road, a particularly scenic country road, to Stimpson Lane. Stimpson Lane is the first right turn intersection you come to after crossing the railroad tracks. Make a right onto Stimpson Lane and ride to the intersection/stop sign. Make a right onto Seashore Road (Route 626) here. Seashore Road turns into Broadway after the railroad tracks. Continue on Broadway to York Avenue. Make a left onto York and go to the Park Boulevard intersection. Make a right onto Park. At the stop sign, make a left. You are now back on West Perry Street. Continue on West Perry Street and follow the Parkway signs. At the West Perry–Lafayette Street intersection, make a left. Just up on your left is the Welcome Center, your starting and ending point.

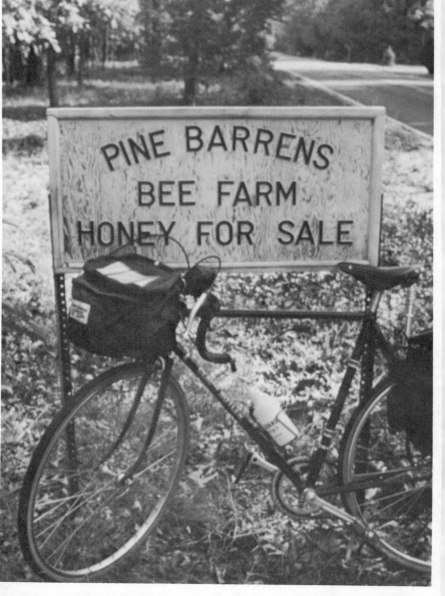

About the Author

Born and raised in New Jersey, travel and sports writer Robert Santelli contributes frequent articles to *New Jersey Monthly, Bicycling* magazine, *Surfer* magazine, and *Caribbean Travel and Life*. A music critic and travel correspondent for the *Asbury Park Press*, he is also the author of *Guide to the Jersey Shore*, published by the Globe Pequot Press.